Quantum City

For my parents,
for Layl,
and
for Beirut

j a n e a l vie

Quantum City

Ayssar Arida

Architectural Press

OXFORD AMSTERDAM BOSTON LONDON NEW YORK PARIS
SAN DIEGO SAN FRANCISCO SINGAPORE SYDNEY TOKYO

Architectural Press
An imprint of Elsevier Science
Linacre House, Jordan Hill, Oxford OX2 8DP
225 Wildwood Avenue, Woburn, MA 01801-2041

First published 2002

British Library Cataloguing in Publication Data
Arida, Ayssar
  Quantum city
  1. City planning   2. Quantum theory
  I. Title
  711.4

Library of Congress Cataloguing in Publication Data
A catalogue record for this book is available from the Library of Congress

ISBN 0 7506 5012 5

For information on all Architectural Press publications visit our
website at www.architecturalpress.com

Design and layout by the author
Composition by Scribe Design, Gillingham, Kent, UK
Printed and bound in Great Britain

Contents

Preface

I should begin with a disclaimer to physicists who might worry that the ideas introduced here have no scientific proof. This book does not make any claims as to the scientific correctness of its postulations; it merely produces a metaphor that borrows language and concepts from quantum theory – or at least from the popularized accounts of it. It creates a 'what if' scenario that wonders how the city would look if viewed through the lens of quantum concepts.

In an introduction to quantum theory basics and its implications, what is often referred to as 'quantum weirdness', for all its uncanny and counterintuitive symptoms, is essential to nudge the reader's expectations from the safe, familiar but limited language of determinism that rules our everyday life. It is also necessary to move up from the comfortable practicalism of our professional practice as urbanists.

What is more crucial in such a subject is to find the right tone of voice to express these ideas, without giving out the impression of 'New Age' rambling. Serious research has unfortunately been burdened with taboo areas, because of their over-use in so-called 'alternative' literature. In May 2001, Amazon.com listed 4096 books in reply to a search for 'quantum' titles, and many seemed to have stuck the word as an afterthought because it seemed so *à la mode*!

In my attempt at bridging two readerships – one interested in 'quantum' subjects and one interested in 'city'-related matters – I have tried to provide as much background information as possible about the development of science and worldviews, and have treated the chapters on urban history in a way that assumes most readers will have a minimum of familiarity with the subject. The book is structured in a way that the reader who is familiar with this territory can selectively skip material up to Chapter 3. However, I strongly suggest you do not skip the introduction to the basics of quantum theory, as the concepts I emphasize might be different from those you might have read elsewhere.

Some readers will find that many issues have been only hinted at, and not developed. A filmmaker friend once told me, 'sometimes what is not on the movie screen is more important than what is; but it is what *is* on the screen that triggers your release from its boundaries'. In this sense, the many unsaid things remain 'out there', and so I hope the novice will take this information as a starting point for further research, while the expert will forgive the simplifications I have had to make to produce as many 'triggers' as possible. The bibliography at the end of the book should provide countless more.

My editors insisted I add a short explanation about the changing text size throughout the book – I assure you it is not a typesetting error. I believe the reason behind this device will become apparent as you go through the book, and as the wave-permeated world I describe becomes clearer.

As for many authors who have eventually written about it, my own 'discovery' of quantum theory and its philosophical implications has been a real epiphany. It included middle-of-the-night insights and weird dreams of quantum antimatter twins ... it has been a most thrilling experience, and I hope the present work will instigate the same curiosity and enthusiasm with which I researched and wrote it.

Acknowledgements

This book would not have been possible without the moral and practical support of my family and friends. In particular I thank Nadia and Richard Arida for their patience, and for the vision and the values they have taught me over the years.

My deepest gratitude goes to Professor Brian Goodey of Oxford Brookes University, for his initial encouragement and for believing with me in the validity of this subject matter. Thanks also to Roger Simmonds, who provided the additional momentum that set this work on course. Layla Shamash, Khalil Norland, Danah Zohar and Ian Marshall have all given me invaluable momentum, particularly Layla, with her beautiful sensitivity and enthusiasm.

As always, my muse Ghalya Saadawi triggered some of the clearest insights. Great thanks go to Grace Azar for the lucky spider, to Inky Hoey and Lea Wood, and to Gabriel Kram for his immaculate friendship and catalysis. Thanks to Modca Café for its wonderful hospitality, many a chapter was written on those immutable red tables!

Thanks to Katherine MacInnes of Architectural Press for her initial leap of faith, Alison Yates for long distance support, and Sue Hamilton for her cheerful patience with all my little whims.

Most importantly, Naji Boutros has my eternal gratitude and friendship, for helping make a great adventure possible.

Introduction

Some mornings I wake up with my head full of rhythms, and rhythms of rhythms, and rhythms of rhythms of rhythms. And to have to speak English is like having to put on a straitjacket.

(Leroy Little Bear 'Sa'ke'j' Henderson)[1]

The purpose of Newspeak was not only to provide a medium of expression for the world-view and mental habits proper to the devotees of Ingsoc, but to make all other modes of thought impossible.

(George Orwell)[2]

I first visited Oxford in 1993, as a tourist with a camera looking for the postcard beauty of a legendary culture of education. I found it in the intriguing orderliness of the place, the gothic grandeur of its formal buildings and the romantic serenity of its landscapes.

When I returned there four years later as a master's student, I felt doubly betrayed. In spite of all the intellectual drama that played itself within the quad walls, a few months within my sojourn I was confronted with the spatial sterility of the place.

Sterility is a shocking word, I admit. We are more willing to qualify Modern functionalist settings with it than places like Oxford. But I assure you, the realization probably shocked me far more than it does you. I had come from Beirut, from all its post-war Mediterranean chaos, where I had been trained as an architect. I had been trained to think of physical order as the ultimate goal of our profession. I had come to the disciplined context of Oxford to be promoted into an urban designer. Against all my expectations, the values I carried as a template in my mind were suddenly put to the test. In order to frame this appropriately for you, I have to take you back and forth between several settings in space and time, so that you can most accurately perceive the arc of the experience that put this book in your hands today.

1997, Oxford. As most other students went home for the semester break, I was left with nothing but the stones of the city, nothing but the physical container of that famous culture the rest of the world envied. Oxford fanatically clung to a predictable homogeneity of form. I felt this exposed her insecurity towards the complexity of her users'* backgrounds. The moment they were all gone, she seemed to recompose her artful veneer only to welcome the buses full of octogenarian American tourists with their Japanese cameras.

*The generic term 'user' will signify throughout the book all people who inhabit, use or move through the urban realm: the 'urbanauts'. This includes local citizens, but also transient students, passers-through, tourists, and so on.

I thought the order of things here would teach me how to 'fix' the chaos of my home country. However, perhaps fuelled by a certain homesickness as my host city emptied of its living users, I realized I would be more comfortable in the physical chaos of Beirut than in the extreme orderliness of this 'beautiful' town. My experience both as a user and as a designer in Beirut had showed me that chaos had a limited manageability, but the excessive blandness of Oxford seemed too sterile. I found total incompatibility, at least on the surface, between the level of stimuli in both places and its relationship to physical form. And the contradicting levels of stimuli in both environments made me doubt my beliefs that what made 'good' urban space was a simplistic vision of static order and homogeneity, and pushed me to look for a middle ground, *a more creative and more dynamic dialogue between order and chaos.*

When I tried to describe what made up the qualities of Beirut, I found it was impossible to do so in the language of my formal education. My conceptual language, the core of my professional expression, betrayed me.

Betrayal is an unforgiving sentiment. It is hard to accept that what you had been counting on would fall short of expressing your problems, let alone solving them. Oxford's stones had perhaps deceived me personally only now, but I felt the betrayal went beyond the stones and beyond me. Every year a plethora of international students, many from non-Western countries, and from diverse cultural and disciplinary backgrounds, return home. There they discover too late the incompatibility of their just-learnt conceptual language with their cities and their lifestyles.

Indeed there were some dimensions missing from the education of urban designers, namely the social, the psychological, and other *subjective* – even *spiritual* – dimensions that one associates with concepts of territoriality, identity, memory, and *meaning* of places and spaces. The interface between social form and physical form varied tremendously from one country to another, through cultural and world-view differences. The Western world had many things to teach developing cities, but there was a lot to be learnt from those cities in return. Yet an under-dimensioned education left us with little insight regarding how to use the experience of different cultures to solve our own problems creatively.

1971–1997, Lebanon. One of the most historically celebrated examples of plural societies ... nineteen different official religious affiliations, four million people on 10 000 square kilometres of sunny coasts, snowy mountains, and green plains: an 'anomaly' in its region, a blessing in disguise. A special case in all the aspects that made up its identity. Lebanon's geography, politics, demographics, ancient and, of course, recent history have all contrived to create one of the world's most contrasted – and contradictory – social and physical environments.

My personal experience was strongly influenced by every aspect of these environments, and to phrase it in the language I will develop for you over the course of this book, you could say that it made my tolerance to the *density of diversity* probably much higher than if I had lived in the English countryside all my life. Born to a Christian father and a Muslim mother, I was exposed to 'both sides of the coin' – and of the story – as I was raised through fifteen years of civil, and less civil, wars. Moving from the city to the suburbs, to and from one or the other of my parents' hometowns (and extended families), to Europe or to the Arabian Gulf, then back to a reconstructing Beirut again, we were constantly fleeing from localized skirmishes, periodically crossing internal and external borders. Palestinians, Israelis, Syrians, Iranians, and Lebanese Muslim Sunnis, Shiites, Druze, Christian Maronites, Fascists, Socialists, and Communists played out their differences on this tiny territory, involving in their turmoil the Americans, the French and the United Nations. Meanwhile, at school and at home we were raised on the stories of this land of mythical Phoenician ancestors, and the histories of Egyptian, Assyrian, Babylonian, Aramean, Hittite, Medean, Persian, Greek, Roman, Arab, Crusader, Ottoman, and French occupations and their cultural legacies ...

Training and practising as an architect since the end of the war in 1989 in Beirut – a city transforming at an incredible speed, but also a city in a continuous tug-of-war between old and new, between East and West, and between regionalism and globalization – has deepened my passion for my city, and for the city in general. War had created the most intense of environments: fighting and *laissez-faire* development had decentralized and re-urbanized more than 80 per cent of the country's population. Most of those displaced preserved many of their rural traditions and worldviews. Squatting in 1950s modernist buildings, they adapted both their physical environment and their lifestyle to fit each other. The layers upon layers of memories and meanings they introduced gave the city an unsettling sense of visual uncertainty, only balanced by an unexpected and buoyant optimism. From Phoenician ruins to those of five-star hotels of the pre-war golden age, Lebanon's history was literally engraved in its bullet-ridden stones, leaving behind an architectural and social landscape of surrealistic strata.

Could the vision of this 'impure', heterogeneous society that experienced and survived a full generation of chaos and uncertainty develop into an emergent urban identity based on diversity? That is the question I was originally interested in answering in my master's thesis in Oxford. But when I realized that the Urban Design *Newspeak* I had been trained in over the previous semester was incapable of such an expression, I almost gave up. I soon found myself searching for an alternative thesis topic.

1997, Oxford. Frustration was setting in as the deadline for the thesis subject proposal came closer ... To relieve the frustration, I needed to forget about urbanism for a while and read other subjects. I took advantage of the term break to access books and resources that would be difficult to find back home.

Several years before arriving in Oxford I was walking one summer through the historical centre of Beirut, under total reconstruction after the fifteen-year war, when I came across an architect friend of mine sitting in the dust of an archeological pit. He was enjoying the sun and a book, waiting for his archeologist girlfriend to finish her work. Seeing me, he invited me to join him. Leaning his back onto a 2000-year-old rock wall, he held in his hand a small book with an intriguing title: *Einstein's Dreams*. He read a passage out loud to me, and I was immediately hooked. Alan Lightman, who teaches physics and writing at MIT, weaves in this book a series of beautiful worlds, *dreams* in the mind of the famous father of relativity and space–time, Albert Einstein. Each dream is extrapolated from strange but possible qualities of time taken to their extreme literal application in a 'real' world, mostly manifested through everyday urban life in parallel versions of Switzerland.

It has since become my fetish book. Back in Oxford, I remembered Alan Lightman and thought I'd look up his other books. The digital catalogue informed me that *Great Ideas in Physics* was available in the university library. Initially disappointed that it sounded like a textbook, I was immediately hooked again, and devoured the pages in one day. The brilliance of it was that it presented the major turning points in science through the character and personal backgrounds of the men and women who brought them about. Somehow understanding *who* the man was made Newton's optimistic determinism or Einstein's relativity theory so much more understandable and fascinating. But by far the most extraordinary story was that of quantum theory, which, unlike the former ideas, was more the work of a multitude of scientists and of decades of interpretation. Its interpretation turned the world of science upside down and inside out, and its application was responsible for all the sophisticated technology of our everyday modern life, from television and lasers to the microchip and digital computers. The history of modern scientific discoveries played itself out like a dramatic thriller, with engaging characters and never-ending surprises and mysteries. With plot twists worthy of the best of science fiction books, the story of quantum physics seemed, in its own right, one of the most remarkable narratives of the twentieth century. As I slowly began to parse apart the worldview elaborated by this revolutionary physics, I was appalled that we had never been taught about all this at school. It was really splendid, and would have made physics classes that much more exciting.

Quantum theory said the world of the infinitely small was made up of *possibilities* and *tendencies*, not of physical certainties. In the strange world of the atom, it was not possible to determine accurately where things were and where they were going at the same time, because they presented themselves as dual-aspect entities. Neither simply *particles* nor simply *waves*, these 'building blocks' of our universe could only be described as *particle~waves*. They were not fixed, dead matter, but *responsive* units that 'decided' which aspect to show the observer at the instant he or she looked at them. Up to the moment of observation, these entities could only be described as *probability waves* and *interconnections* that dynamically linked their possible position and their possible action. What was more, not only could a subatomic entity be in different places at the same time, it also actually behaved as if it *really were* in different places. Its probability wave filled all space and time and gave it certain qualities, which other entities' waves *interfered* with to produce new *emergent* qualities, and on and on. Quantum theory reconnected the world and finally recombined *objectivity* and *subjectivity* into one model of reality, clashing with all that classical thought believed the world to be.

As the semester break was winding to a close, this might have been the end of that story. A fascinating narrative, a compelling theory, a revolutionary way of looking at the world; marvellous entertainment, but not my discipline at all. And yet, the strangeness of that world began to unfold into reality.

Several days later, still wrestling subconsciously with my relationship to Beirut and Oxford, to my programme and to my thesis, something happened while I was sleeping. Like Newton's apple, like Einstein's flash of light, it came to me in a dream. I woke up in the middle of the night, grabbed a piece of paper and scribbled: 'Quantum UD' – Quantum Urban Design. What suddenly became clear to me was that the world of quantum theory, in all its strangeness and changeability, could in fact provide a metaphorical language applicable to urban design.

Quantum theory seemed to describe a world of *complementary dualities*, of both/and values, of uncertainty, of choices at all scales, of interactive relationships, emergent qualities and of sustainable vibrant ecologies ... a language that described best the complex artefact that is the city: the *urbs* AND the *civitas*, the stones AND the emotions*. The language needed to describe the chaos, uncertainty, complexity, heterogeneity and subjectivity of life in the city had been there all along. Scientists had been forced to create it as the only means of describing what their empirical experience at the heart of matter was showing them, but we had never been taught this language.

The book that you now hold in your hands is the result of several years of grappling with the ideas that emerged from this original insight. It is an attempt to borrow some conceptual formulations from quantum theory, and to use it as a background metaphor to describe the urban realm. In the search for concepts better adapted to the paradigm that has come to affect most of our production at the dawn of the millennium, I will attempt to map the city in a language that is more deeply applicable to the complexity we observe to be operating in 'vibrant' space.

What I want to share with you is the sense of excitement, the utter dumbfoundedness that occurred in that epiphanous moment when I

*Saint Isidore of Seville (c. AD 560–636) traced in his Etymologies the origins of the word city to different sources: the urbs (or stones of a city), laid for 'practical reasons of shelter, commerce and warfare'; and civitas, 'the emotions, rituals and convictions that take form in a city'.[3] Thus, the urbs and the civitas could also be defined as the physical and the cultural (or political), or, in the language of quantum theory, as the particle and the wave aspects that make up the city.

discovered, suddenly and to my great surprise, that an eloquent language had just opened itself up to me. It finally allowed me to express something that had always been buried intuitively in my perception of the world, and which I had been unable to articulate before. I hope you will join me in my curiosity, as we unfold and explore this alternative way of looking at the city and describing it. It is a way much closer to our intuitive thought processes, and one that will hopefully lead us to some qualitatively different conclusions.

1 worldviews and the city

We are the music makers,
And we are the dreamers of dreams ...
Yet we are the movers and shakers
Of the world forever it seems.

We, in the ages lying,
In the buried past of the earth,
Built Nineveh with our sighing,
And Babel itself with our mirth;
And o'erthrew them with prophesizing
To the old of the new world's worth;
For each age is a dream that is dying,
Or one that is coming to birth.

(Arthur William Edgar O'Shaughnessy, *Ode*)

> In this world ... time flows more slowly the farther from the centre of the earth. ... Once the phenomenon was known, a few people, anxious to stay young, moved to the mountains. Now all houses are built on Dom, the Matterhorn, Monte Rosa, and other high ground. It is impossible to sell living quarters elsewhere. ... People most eager to live longest have built their houses on the highest stilts.
>
> (A. Lightman)[1]

2001, Beirut. Walking through the city centre again ... a perfectly drawn grid now replaces whatever was left of the historic core, ransacked and destroyed in 1975–1976, and squatted until the early 1990s by all the displaced have-nots. They had appropriated what was supposed to be the no-man's land cutting the city in two. Living and working in the ruins between the landmines and the wild vegetation, they benefited from the weapons upgrade of the belligerents that had transformed the street fighting into long-distance artillery warfare. Since 1993, a giant real estate company in charge of reconstruction had been erasing their traces to give the centre back its 'role', but succeeding so far only where war had failed – making it a real no-man's land. The tabula rasa that has wilfully replaced the traditional fabric has spared a few buildings, now pristinely restored. But life is taking its time to come back to what was the commerce and entertainment heart of the Middle East. Not too long ago street merchants still sold postcards and posters of this place in all its pre-war glory. Now even they are not allowed to bring old memories onto this 'Ancient City for the Future', as an artist's rendering of this site proudly proclaims ...

The clearing of the old fabric was based on a master plan devised by a sole aging architect with a virulent combination of Beaux Arts, modernist and postmodernist streaks. Legend has it he locked himself up in Cairo and drafted the plan, pulling in together two avenues wider than the Champs Elysées, twin towers reminiscent of the World Trade Center, a Manhattan-style artificial island reclaimed on the sea, and 40-storey semi-circular glass office towers topped with red-roof tiles 'to give the approaching planes a bird's-eye view of a Mediterranean city'. Eight-lane under-passes and overpasses cut through the old fabric as if it were never there. The whole was to be executed through an expropriation by a single (private) real estate company of all the property rights of the city centre, in return for shares. Needless to say, it was horrific.

The plan and the process fuelled many debates, but while the skilled debaters fought over melan-cholia of past and melancholia of future, a superb fleet of modern bulldozers left nothing to debate over. Under pressure, the new owners of the Beirut Central District (BCD) dumped the old plan and brought in a new team of international urban designers. They had to work with what was now there: nothing. The result is a very politically correct New Urbanism master plan, as rigid as can be, and as foreign to twenty-first century Beirut as can be – at least morphologically. It is amusing to read an American criticizing a Scotsman* on the issue of the post-war reconstruction of the Beirut Central District:

> Angus Gavin's referents for development are Haussmann or Regency England. The combination of imports is

*Angus Gavin is the 'Urban Planning Advisor to the Chairman' of Solidere, the real estate company in charge of the development of the Beirut Central District. Michael Stanton is Chairman of the architecture department at the American University of Beirut. The essay in question is from Gavin, 1998.

alarming in this melding of European Colonial prototypes and American New Urbanist formats. [... His] essay is both colonial in its view and 18th century in its tone. One can almost hear Mr Shenstone's raptures to Mr Thomson over some particularly delightful episode of arranged landscape or new bit of Chinoiserie. Admiration of 'views' and 'a more Anglo-Saxon search for context and cultural continuity that seemed more appropriate' calls forth a colonial Pastoral that fits the attitude of the entire project. Even 'the Orientalist painters of the last century' are seen as inspiration.[2]

But few are complaining now; the powers that be have chosen the physical form of the future city centre, and what remains to come in is its soul, hopefully through some symbiotic contamination with the rest of the city – the spatial, the social and the historical hinterlands. The clearing of the modern ruins has at least created the opportunity for ancient ones to surface. The BCD is claimed to be the largest urban archaeology site in the world and, from the sight of it, it seems one of the most multi-layered. It is said that Beirut was completely destroyed and rebuilt seven times in history; maybe that is where it gets its impalpable vibes ...

I hadn't come back to this archaeology pit since 1994. I decided to return here to see if I could find new inspiration for the first part of this book, about the world-views of ancient civilizations. I think this is where I first discovered *Einstein's Dreams*[1] with its multiple worlds created from multiple visions of time. The worlds of the book were all different lifestyles in the same Swiss cities, lifestyles based on beliefs transformed into streets and squares and houses on wheels or on stilts ... weren't the different cities of the ancient civilizations just that: different visions of the world made into form?

Modern Beirut is a little more than a century old, but this territory has been continuously inhabited for more than six millennia. The sea-faring Phoenicians, merchants extraordinaire of antiquity, had developed a number of independent city-states along the eastern shore of the Mediterranean, ports of exchange between the empires of the east and those of the west. Beirut was one of the lesser city-states; Byblos to the North, Sidon and Tyre to the south were more powerful and influential, and their ports exported rare glassware, luxurious purple silk and cedar wood to Egypt and Greece. The Romans, who captured the region in 64 BC and established Julia Augusta Felix Berytus – 'Julia's Joy' – as a Roman colony in 14 BC, secured this city's place in antiquity*. The ruins under my feet are thought to be the vestiges of the main Law Academy of the Empire.

*Julia was the daughter of the Emperor Augustus.

The Roman Empire

27 BC–AD 395. The Romans were what we would call in modern jargon 'control freaks'. After romanizing all of Italy, the warriors–aesthetes spread into an empire that would link up all the Mediterranean and beyond. By the time they defeated the Greeks in 146 BC, they had developed a strongly materialistic worldview that was also largely tolerant and pluralistic: in a way, Romans were practical people – as long as the different peoples that came under their control respected their authority and paid their dues to the Empire, they were allowed to keep their beliefs and culture intact, even as they became Roman citizens. In fact, it was the Romans themselves that let their own culture be enriched by others. In particular, they inherited from the Greeks their philosophy and their quest for natural order, then filtered them through their administrative vision and made them into a practical and successful model.

Establishing law 'as the basis of civil and military administration', they expressed it through rational ordered town planning, inherited from Alexander the Great under whom town planning 'superseded the instinctive and irrational planning of the Greeks'.[3]

> For the Romans, the beautiful was that which reflected the underlying principle of their Law. This law has its goal achieving the greatest possible internal coherence of society, and all their principles of efficiency derived from this end rather than from mere function.[4]

The Roman lust for power meant that the relation of their buildings to the natural landscape was generally one of dominion, but their equal love for law and order produced masterpieces of aesthetic harmony of opposites: unlike the Greek search for poise, theirs was a search for a creative tension between order and wild nature. Their belief in law and self-righteousness created some of the Western world's most magnificent and enduring examples of technical prowess combined with a deep respect for nature.

In their civic environments, Romans were more engineers than architects, and more urban planners than philosophers. They borrowed the universal form of the Greek temple for almost all their typologies, both secular and sacred, yet thanks to their less zealous relation to philosophy they eventually developed extreme variations into baths, schools, houses, and all the elements of urban life. Concentrating on rational organization rather than philosophical implications, they were nevertheless able to stamp all their colonies with similar organizational rules: an outer boundary would be set, then a centre created at the intersection of two perpendicular main roads, the *cardo* and the *decumanus*. At the centre the public forum was placed. From this initial set of origin and axis, a Cartesian grid of secondary streets and sub-centres developed.

This system was in fact the same they used for the layout of military encampments, and was the logical next step in the transformation of the camp into a permanent settlement. It created a strong contrast (and therefore a strong message) between the Roman New Order and the generally unplanned territories and villages they came to conquer. Yet with the exception of a few cities in North Africa, most Roman colonies were boring diminutives of what Rome itself dreamt to be. The rigorous repetition of the planning system as a physical expression of imperial law seemed designed to overcome the frustration of not being able to shape the capital itself. Unlike the colonies, Rome had been forming over centuries into a dense living organism that was difficult to perturb. Imposing spatial order became a matter of localized interventions that would axialize urban space in piecemeal growth.

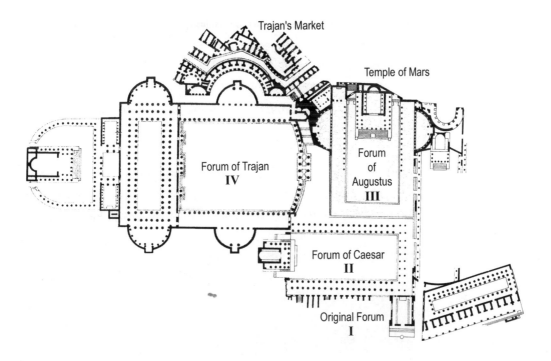

Between 46 BC and AD 113, successive emperors built a constellation of forums to extend the congested historical centre of the capital (Figure 1.1). Their scale and expression parallel the state of the Empire at the time they were built. Julius Caesar's was the first extension, and is easily the most rigorous and military-like. It speaks of the grandeur of the father of the Empire, a military genius who became the first emperor to be deified in Roman history. It is designed as a simple rectangle of perfect proportions, surrounded by three porticoes and

Figure 1.1
The Imperial Forums of Rome.

crowned on one of the short sides with a temple to Caesar himself. Less than 50 years later, Augustus followed with a forum set perpendicularly to Caesar's. Augustus was one of Rome's greatest emperors: when he wasn't establishing colonies for the joy of his daughters, he would be reorganizing the state and building or restoring more than 90 temples within a few years. Yet probably out of respect for the still immense legacy of Caesar, he kept the design of his forum very much in the same style as his predecessor, and only added an *exidrae* (half-circular space) at each side of the rectangle. A vow made before the victory at Philippi in 42 BC dedicated the temple flanking the forum to the god of war, Mars. In a common case of urban design choices, worldviews and politics feeding back into each other, 'the forum became the cult centre of Roman military power. It was there that the senate decided upon questions of war and peace, and there that statues commemorated conquering generals.'[5]

By the time Apollodorus of Damascus set out to build his forum dedicated to Trajan (in AD 113), the Empire was at its peak.

The Pax Romana had spread to the confines of the territory, bringing political stability and economic wealth for over two centuries. The forum of Trajan fits well into the state of affairs of the Empire: a

Figure 1.2
The second century Internet.

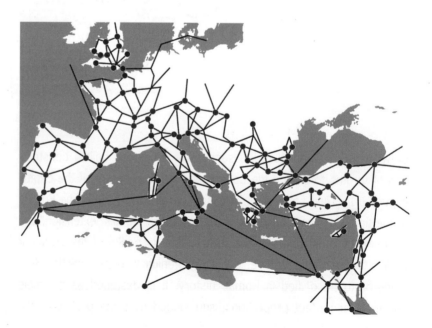

grandiose, architecturally diverse complex almost four times the size of Caesar's initial forum, it incorporates a basilica, a library, an impressive temple, and a multi-level market of 150 shops and offices, selling goods from the four corners of the Roman world. The diversity of landscapes and cultures covered by the Empire had pushed the Romans to build an unprecedented network of roads and aqueducts that linked all the colonies together, creating a constant flow of goods and culture in all directions (Figure 1.2). The web eventually exceeded 100 000 kilometres, and beyond trade, it 'carried Roman culture from Scotland to the Sahara, and irreversibly altered civilization'[6] – the second century's version of the Internet.

This bridging of cultures was as social and temporal as it was spatial: 330 years after it crucified Jesus, Rome embraced Christianity as its official religion. By doing so, it created a double historical bridge between Greek philosophy and what was to become the medieval worldview, and between classical Greece and what was to be called the Renaissance.

The Classical Greek polis

480–30 BC. Compared to the Romans, the ancient Greeks were much more spiritual and inquisitive. Over the centuries of Greek history, the details of religion were more a matter of individual philosophizing than that of an official state vision. Yet the background belief in a divine pantheon formed a strong metaphor for the development of literature, drama and architecture. This society of warriors, politicians and philosophers had a highly evolved organic worldview that strongly reflected itself in all its art and construction:

> The Ancient Greek could use his or her eyes to see the complexities of life. The temples, markets, playing fields, meeting places, walls, public sanctuary, and paintings of the ancient city represented the culture's values in religion, politics, and family life.[7]

In his extraordinary *The Conscience of the Eye*, written in 1990, Richard Sennett even suggests that their places could also give out the experience of remorse or promote democracy (such as the assembly or the agora) while their gymnasiums taught them 'the moral dimensions of sexual desire', and he links that to the clarity with which they saw the fullness of life, as their *inner* and *outer*, their subjective and objective realms, were strongly unified. The ancient Greeks' philosophy of morals and aesthetics that reflected itself on their behaviour and their environment was strongly influenced by Plato's Realm of Forms, and Aristotle's Golden Mean.

Plato believed in an ideal world of Forms that was the backbone of all perceived reality. He believed that the only way towards the comprehension of the divine order of the Ideal Forms was through contemplation and reason. His own pupil Aristotle, on the other hand, found that the road to knowledge was through a more empirical study of the earthly world. The complementary thought of these two great men was the continuation of a tradition of oscillating philosophies that went down for centuries in ancient Greece, and was eventually to influence the expression of Judeo-Christianity and the Western worldview and science. 'Plato was the artificer, Aristotle the ecologist, in a world in which individual and thinking man had arrived.'[8]

The Greeks designed their monuments according to this worldview. Their belief in the central importance of man to nature, both physically and mentally, led to the anthropomorphic systems of proportion being complemented by rational and philosophical systems such as Platonist geometry or Pythagorian harmonics. Unlike the Romans, who adopted a self-boasting architecture and sculpture, their best structures showed 'poise' and 'centredness'. They were humanly proportioned, and positioned according to their symbolical and theological value, as a recognition and expression of the spirit of places, mountains, hills and islands. Temples responded to the genius loci of the landscape with no general apparent order but with clarity of form; simultaneously, priests inaugurated cities, as 'the rite of the founding of a town touches on one of the great commonplaces of religious experience'.[9]

Miletus, a small city at the edge of the Ionian peninsula, produced many philosophers who were at the roots of Greek materialism. Between

600 BC and 550 BC, Thales, Anaximander and Anaximenes all developed philosophies that looked for the elementary components of the physical universe in nature. That same city was to be re-planned around 475 BC by a thought now influenced by Platonic rationalism. Hippodamus, master-planner of Miletus, is conventionally thought to be the first to have used the grid as an expression of the rationality of civilized life. A dozen centuries later, a similar concern for a rationalization of space produced the first American grids. In fact, for the fathers of the USA, the Greeks and the Romans were to be a favourite model: the confederation of Greek Republics was often cited as a paradigm of perfect administration, and clear parallels have been drawn between the Senate and the House of Representatives on one hand and the Patrician and the Plebeian legislative bodies of Rome on the other.[10] It is thus no wonder that most governmental buildings in the USA favour a Greco-Roman classical architecture as a significant of authority – a search for legitimacy in ancient roots manifested as a literal translation between the two worldviews' physical output. Just think of the architecture of the American Courts of Justice, and remember that the symbol of Justice, the statue of the blindfolded woman with the scales, is none other than the Greek goddess of Justice, Themis daughter of Zeus ...

In contrast to their New World emulators (and even their Roman emulators), the Ancient Greeks did not claim to subjugate their territory. Both morphologically and functionally, Greek cities were laid according to symbolic and symbiotic relations with their sites; elevated grounds became sacred, while purely shaped freestanding temples unobtrusively completed sacred natural settings. Within cities such as Athens, a sacred domain was reserved for the gods. The temple on the Acropolis became the symbol of universal order through geometry. Striving for perfection through form, it seemed more a laboratory to experiment with geometry and optics than a place of worship. It was designed for the human gaze more than for the god's appeasement; the Greek temple's symbolism was more aesthetic and visual than spatial. In a sense, it was as much a temple to the intellect of Man as to the gods, a stark contrast with the worldview of the Egyptians, who deified the pharaoh before building a temple to his might.

Pharaonic Egypt

c. 2660 BC. Almost four centuries after the unification of Upper and Lower Egypt into one country, Imhotep, the scribe, priest, architect and vizier of Pharaoh Zoser, introduced architecture in stone. It was crucial for the true expression of a worldview that was to rule over the land of the Nile for over three millennia.

Faced with a land of impressive flatness, scorched by a relentless sun and rhythmed by an inexorable river, the ancient Egyptians developed a mythology centred on the elements of their environment. From 3000 BC until the early days of the Christian era, the Nile civilization adopted a truly organic worldview. All aspects of daily life were based on a set of beliefs shared by the great majority of the population, and shaped by a mixture of religion and science.

While religion deified the Nile and the sun, science – in fact inextricable from religion – taught the Egyptians of ways to manage their lives accordingly. The sun and the river provided them with life and its rhythms, seasons for agriculture, and periodical rituals. Their whole culture revolved around what their priests–scientists told them of the world: the pharaoh was a demigod, brother of the sun god Ra, hence his unlimited power and the hierarchical society structure below him, all the way down to the slave workers. Afterlife and omnipotent gods required pyramids, tombs and temples. Such large-scale projects could only be ordered and managed by the theologists–architects; slavery made their construction possible. The belief in the superiority of the afterlife over daily existence thus allowed extraordinary expenses in wealth, time and human lives toward what would appear today as futile gigantism.

The pharaoh, sole master of the land and representative on earth of the perfect realm of the gods, organized the distribution of resources and built physical order into a formerly chaotic environment. The vertical thrust of the pyramids and obelisks and the axiality of the temples and palaces can be seen as an attempt to reinterpret godly order and additional (vertical) dimensions over a flat, two-dimensional land that

stretched endlessly; it is also a graphic need to represent continuity between earthly life and the afterworld, and between the underworld and the sphere of the heavens (Figure 1.3).

Figure 1.3
Egyptian landscape.

After centuries mastering building in bricks and wood, stone became the material of choice for the construction of all sacred structures, to ensure the continuity of the new order for all eternity. It allowed the jump from the stepped pyramid developed from the basic *mastaba*, to the perfect pyramid with flat granite-faced sides. The form itself was a translation of the image of the 'primordial hill illuminated by the first rays of the sun at the time of the creation of the world' [11] and then became a representation of the sunrays shining down on the land.

In contrast, secular constructions such as dwellings and markets were built of cheap, short-lasting mud bricks. In terms of form and urban design, again it was the symbolism of religion combined with the knowledge of astronomers that fixed Egyptian settlements and positioned their axes according to precise astrological directions. The social order, tightly connected to the hierarchical religious structure, segregated the secular constructions in terms of size and density, even though typologically dwellings remained similar to each other and mostly differed only in scale.

The holistic and ecological worldview of the ancient Egyptians is clearly manifested through the interaction of their three modes of existence: temporal, spatial and social. Their landscape – the flat desert, two-dimensional and unlimited in space, and the Nile, periodic, recurrent and predictable – organized Time. The tombs, palaces, and temples were axial, symmetrical, and symbolic; eternal in Time but fixed in space, these sacred structures organized Space. Finally, the dwellings, markets, prisons and all the secular functions of the city – organic, temporary and temporal – organized Society.

All architectural choices were made by the religious authorities, at all scales – from the location of the new city, its layout and that of its temples and tombs, to the very decoration on the walls. For example, with the growing influence of the scribes around 2500 BC, interiors of pyramids became more sophisticated, with the walls becoming more than ever true 'pyramid texts', stone-carved archives of the knowledge and history of the civilization. These were not merely aesthetic decoration; they were real 'magic formulae' that would open up the world of the afterlife for the dead, and welcome the gods on their visit to earth. Sun worship was expressed in open courts and obelisks that contrasted with the inner sanctums representing a hidden, mysterious deity. As emphasis oscillated between one and the other of those two opposing principles of Egyptian religion over the centuries, so did the physical form. During the early days of the New Kingdom (c. 1552–1070 BC), emphasis was on the hidden deity, and so temples emphasized the inner sanctums over the sun courts – eventually taken to an extreme with the building of the first temples carved into the rock, as with Queen Hatchepsut's fascinating temple at Deir el Bahri, which majestically steps up into the cliff.

In 1364 BC Akhenaton tried to impose what was perhaps the first historical attempt at monotheism, refuting all the Egyptian gods but one, the sun-disc Aton. He settled his new capital at Tell-el-Amarna, hundreds of kilometres away from his ancestors' capital Thebes, to signify his break with tradition. He needed a new city because he needed a physical expression of his new religion. As he travelled the desert up the Nile looking for a site, he came to a point where the morning sun rose from right behind a double hill, precisely as Egyptian myth described genesis. Akhetaten – 'the horizon of Aten' – was built from scratch, and was characterized by a rather regular grid aligned with the Nile. At its centre was the great temple of Aton: a gigantic solar court enclosed by a high stone wall, unusually decorated with colours, as if better to express the beauty of the sun's light. In the court was a relatively small structure for the hidden deity, which only the pharaoh himself could access. This contrasted greatly with the typical Egyptian temples, where the procession from sun court to inner sanctum was much more gradual, going through a peristyle court, a hypostyle hall and an inner temple before getting to the sanctuary that held the statue of the god.

In a way, by abandoning transition spaces, the heretic pharaoh's temple expressed the dualism that he had suddenly instated on the land. The new religion seemed to the Egyptians too exclusive, as if the sun only shone for the pharaoh and his family. Of course the priests weren't happy either with their loss of power, and so with the death of Akhenaton his city was destroyed by its own people, and its ruins were covered with chalk as if to erase all memory of this anomalous worldview. Ironically, it was probably that action that preserved Akhetaten for discovery by modern archeologists …

Whatever the fate of Akhetaten, the rest of the constructions of the ancient Egyptians conveyed such an impressive culture that its essence remained untouched over millennia, even as Egypt lost its independence. 'The power of Egyptian culture and its intellectual authority again imposed itself on the various invaders. Libyan, Nubian, Persian, Greek or Roman invaders ruling over the conquered country adopted Pharaonic customs.'[11] Some even took the customs back home in the form of town planning and architecture.

(From my archeology pit, I look up to the only pre-war building that has remained on the side of what was Martyr's Square, and I smile to myself: the mythical Cinema Opera is a very elegant limestone structure built in the 1930s … in a frankly neo-Egyptian deco style. It is being refurbished as a Virgin Megastore (Figure 1.4).)

Figure 1.4
The Cinema Opera building in the Beirut Central District, now the Virgin Megastore.

Some of the most beautifully preserved temples in the traditional pharaonic style were still being built well into the fifth century AD. The Greek and Roman rulers that commissioned them were represented on their walls in the same style and costume as the first pharaoh of Egypt, three-and-a-half millennia before. A unique worldview was thus perpetuated by buildings that acted as memory banks for their successors: 'Their walls were covered even more systematically with scenes and texts, as if they had a duty to preserve the achievements and the spirit of Egyptian civilization.'[11]

It was only Christianity's intolerance to paganism that ended all that by transforming the temples into churches, and eventually physically replacing them in the times of St Isidore of Seville in the sixth century.

The Christian city of God

AD 330+. Constantine the Great converted the Roman Empire to Christianity and moved the capital to Constantinople in AD 330. The Empire crumbled and was finally dismantled in AD 395, marking the beginning of the Byzantine era. In those formative years, new buildings were erected to serve the functions of the new religion (Figure 1.5). The first basilicas appeared in Rome; the church of the Nativity in Bethlehem, the Holy Sepulchre on Golgotha, and the church of the Resurrection in Jerusalem created physical bookmarks on the land of Christ. The same period saw the development of the first monasteries, which eventually became centres of learning. The new faith and the new architectural ingredients formed a whole new concept of the city.

Figure 1.5
The Hagia Eirene in Constantinople (modern Istanbul), originally built in the 4th century AD by Constantine the Great and rebuilt extensively in the 6th century by Emperor Justinian I (copyright Stavrides Photius).

St Augustine wrote *City of God*, after the sack of Rome by barbarian hordes in AD 410. In it he defined the philosophy of protective blind faith, separating between two conflicting worlds, that of Faith and that of everyday life. In doing that, he:

> ... laid the theological foundation for a city whose architecture and urban forms would give the restless spirit a home. ... This was because Augustine believed in 'religious vision' as a concrete, perceptual act, not simply as a verbal metaphor. 'Religious vision' would lead, eventually, to an inner life that took life in glass and stone.[11]

This vision *literally* blinded the faithful, and therefore they had to surrender completely to God's promise of security. A vision with ultimately concrete socio-political implications: 'You are promised that you will be taken care of, if only you submit, if you do your duty to bishop or king or parent. Vision, then, leads the wanderer to a house of submission in which the pains of exposure come to an end.'[12]

Two centuries later, St Isidore of Seville (560–636) devoted himself to actually realizing this vision of a Christian city in real glass and stone. In his *Etymologies*, he defined the city as made up of *urbs* and of *civitas*, the physical and the cultural-political components. Unlike the early fathers of the Church, who saw no harm in living in the remnants of a pagan Rome, Isidore tore down old temples and constructed a true Christian city. As most cities of the Roman Empire were falling into ruin, only the belief in the Church and its protective hierarchy could permit the growth and development of such cities as Paris or Milan.

> In these circumstances only a very strong set of beliefs, of values deeply and passionately held, could serve as an ideal of renewal ... a devotion that would sustain generation after generation of mason and carpenter [... to build] that ideal of the inside, in which the Children of God were made safe from the street of [...] difference.[12]

As Sennett reminds us, then, a key catalyst behind the proliferation of the Christian network of cities (at least spiritually) was the Church's obligation to provide shelter. Most interestingly, this view brings out the real underlying order behind the planning of those cities we sometimes regard as unplanned and disordered, but that we nevertheless look back onto as 'pleasant' and 'harmonious'. Haphazard streets, laid out without reference to buildings lining them, variable in width and direction, responded in reality to a different set of rules: 'The medieval builders were masons and carpenters, not philosophers. As Christians, they knew only that secular space had to look unlike sacred space.'[12] This simple rule transformed Augustine's religious faith into physical form: secular streets and buildings are put together haphazardly, inefficiently, while the churches 'were carefully sited, their construction precise, their design [and effect] elaborately calculated'. Even at the small scale of architecture, 'engineering became part of religious effort, precision took on a spiritual meaning'.

Through *discontinuity*, rather than *emphasis*, medieval planners drew attention to the Church as the spiritual centre, the secure refuge. In other words, they used a *spatial* gesture, rather than an *architectural* or simply *formal* gesture to signify the importance of the edifice, and to symbolize the worldview. A worldview difficult to represent today:

> ...again, it offends modern common sense in turn to speak of building at random; however, permitting squares and houses to sprout randomly created the necessary contrast to make clarity speak as an experience of faith ... making place sacred through definitions that contrasted to secular irregularity became a mark of Western urbanism.[12]

Yet everything about the church building contrasted with its surroundings, beyond the mere location: upon entering the sacrosanct space, the believer was overwhelmed with the whole atmosphere of the inside. Perfect proportions of the structure and the openings, the careful placement of stained glass and statues to activate the light and the shadows, the flickering candles, the smell of wax and incense, everything contrasted with the emptiness of the outside, its clattering noise and the stench of the open sewers.

The Christian worldview not only affected the urban form – the *urbs* – but also its functioning – the *civitas*. For example, in the open, empty no-man's-land separating the cathedral from the rest of the secular city, not even trade could be practised: 'Though the bulk and weight of church buildings generated shade and protection from wind, which might have facilitated commerce, the [symbolic] gulf between the sacred and the secular forbade such practical use'. Instead, this empty 'locality of immunity' was where 'all those in need gained the right to be cared for', a transitional space/period before they could be offered sanctuary within the actual walls of the cathedral. 'Here beggars established themselves, here the still-living victims of plague were carried from their houses and laid upon the ground. Here also was the place where babies were abandoned.'[12]

(In the desolate void of the Beirut Central District, churches, mosques and synagogues were the only structures untouchable by the bulldozers. When the socio-religious realities proved tougher than real estate ambitions*, the urbanists in charge of the reconstruction reversed the historical tide of morphology, surrounding each religious building with a no-build perimeter – an absurdly atemporal 'locality of immunity' in an age where commercial buildings dwarf churches ....)

*In Lebanon, religious *waqf*, or church properties, cannot be expropriated by the government.

With time, the Christian worldview changed and adopted less radical stances of separation, namely through the reconciliatory work of St Thomas Aquinas (1225–1274):

> Aquinas joined two methods. Reason was no longer conceived as the nemesis of Faith. Neither was Philosophy the enemy of Theology. Instead, Aquinas joined the two by claiming that both were paths to a single truth: God exists.[13]

Aquinas' synthesis came with a series of socio-economical changes that were sweeping throughout medieval Europe, bringing change and added freedom. One of the nuances of the new Christian worldview was the acceptance of entertainment and rational knowledge to spread through vernacular literature: *La Chanson de Roland*, the *Kaiserchronik*, the *Canterbury Tales*, the *Decameron*, and Dante's *Divine Comedy* were all composed around that fertile period. An effect on urban space can be seen through the cultural activities that now came out of the church walls and into the street, activating the no-man's land: with the pagan rituals of Greek drama a safe historical distance behind, plays themed around Christian virtue and perilous sin were allowed to enliven the streets, as the Church realized it could use theatre for its own propaganda. The old functions were relegated to the back spaces, as the concept of church as sanctuary, and as a centre for both physical and spiritual healing, eventually combined with that of the monasteries to create a new function and typology in the city: the hospital.

By the end of the thirteenth century, the new approach to Faith and Reason permitted another very important development: the establishment of universities in Paris, Oxford, Berlin, Padua, and Bologna. The effect of the new typologies on urban morphology, economics and politics is exemplified in the layout of Oxford or Cambridge, for instance, and the development of education as an industry that could catalyse local economies. The new centres for learning also opened the way for doubting the authority of the Catholic Church, but not religion itself. This led to the spread of heretical movements throughout Europe, a period of spiritual and political turmoil, then a reaction to it that expressed itself best through the arts: the Renaissance.

Renaissance and baroque urbatecture

14th C+. The newly emancipated and enriched society of the fourteenth century looked back at the previous times of turmoil and saw only darkness. The intellectuals of the *Quattrocento* sought the antithesis to those 'Dark Ages' (in reality a major transitional and formative period) in the revival of ancient Greek and Roman values.

> There they found thinkers who had similar interests and who had wrestled perhaps, with identical problems. The medieval synthesis had grown formal; too compartmentalized, too confining. It was too damn logical. Too systematic. Too Aristotelian. And the Renaissance reacted strongly against the medieval matrix – against all that pigeon-holing.[13]

The wars and the epidemics had brought back the attention from the World of God to that of Man and Nature. During the Quattrocento, art and architecture, poetry and politics, science and economics, all focused on human potential for excellence. 'The new worldview – at least part of it – would be fashioned according to the reigning two ideals of the period: individuality and self-sufficiency.' Humanism was back with a vengeance, after the fourteen centuries the Church had spent erasing this concern with the temporal world. In Kreis' words: 'St Augustine would have been most disappointed. If his artificial dichotomy of the Two Worlds meant anything, it was that the City of God was superior in all ways to the City of Man.'[13]

It is in such a context that Renaissance artists and builders set about redesigning their cities. The focus now went towards the creation of 'beautiful' and 'meaningful' public spaces that were in themselves works of art, and that would reaffirm the city of man. 'The eye, by changing perspective', Sennett tells us, 'can change how the world looks', and it was the invention of perspective that was to provide a perfect geometric tool for the layout of streets that would enhance a sense of movement and discovery:

> Recourse to perspective as a model for urban design suggested to [Renaissance] planners a new way to establish the meaning of a street line leading to a centre – a meaning far different than the medieval sanctuary, though equally charged with importance. The centres created through perspective were places in which, it was thought, people would keep moving and look searchingly around them. In these centres, discoveries would occur.[14]

After yet another sack of Rome, this time in 1527 by the armies of Emperor Charles V, Pope Sixtus V set about transforming the remains of the Renaissance city into Europe's first baroque capital. His plan linking the seven pilgrimage sites of Rome through a network of perspective-enhanced streets and obelisks at nodes is a famous example of the new perspectival approach. The difference with medieval planning can be seen in the disregard of the latter for the real-life human experience of the believer, where only his soul was important, as all he had to do was have faith. 'The divide from earlier planning was simple: [medieval builders] determined by building high so people would know where churches were; Pope Sixtus V established how to get there.'[14]

> The man of God, resolute in his dogmatic opinions and asceticism – fashioned by centuries of Church domination and synthesized by Aquinas – had, by the fourteenth century, become godlike himself. The new Faust was, in the end, destined to make his own future, to make his own history.[13]

The new worldview tried to emulate the ancient Roman and Greek values, and inevitably studied and copied their architecture and urban forms. Thanks to the new empowering discoveries and realizations such as perspective, Copernicus's heliocentric model, or the discovery of the New World, with its strange lands and customs, more creative extremes were inspired. The new optimism brought with it extraordinary urban development. The Church of Rome was as rich as ever, especially with the expansion of the mercantile networks; political rulers were intellectuals and humanists who spent fortunes on building schools and palaces. Soon the new attitude would bring about the Scientific Revolution, and the success of its ideas would feed back and push the new paradigm further forward.

2

science
and worldviews

Since the beginning of civilization, man has looked upon his world through the spectacles of his beliefs. From *Homo Sapiens* to *Homo Cyber*, our social, physical, and personal worlds have been shaped by what we know and what we believe, both consciously and unconsciously. What we know of the world has in turn been influenced by our social, political, and cultural structures. In prehistory, this knowledge of the world was the fruit of experience, but also that of superstition and imagination. This set of superstitions developed into rituals then religion, and religion grew in power until it fused with politics and developed 'official' worldviews. In parallel, human curiosity was growing in power until it was formalized as philosophy, then as 'science'. Science grew in the shadow of religion, and for a long time its sole purpose seemed to be to prove the 'official' worldview.

When ancient civilizations opened their eyes to the world, they saw nature's forces as erratic, unfathomable entities that could only be gods. Some looked more closely than others and saw that nature had a certain logic, which, although beyond their understanding, was definitely worth studying. Magic and science overlapped in a series of beliefs with direct practical implications, from medicinal healing to social rituals to architecture and symbolism. Unfortunately the mere amassing of knowledge could not stop the decline of civilizations, or the attacks of nearby barbarians. Civilizations thus peaked and waned, each with its own set of values and beliefs, of scientific knowledge, and its own worldviews.

Every once in a while some overzealous 'scientist' shook the 'official' worldview, and every once in a while that scientist was neither killed nor stifled. Eventually knowledge became increasingly available to the general public, through an increase of literacy and the development of basic forms of mass media ... and some ideas slowly grew to be the seeds of worldviews that bypassed or redefined the religious beliefs towards more temporal and material relationships with the immediate universe.

As authority became more secular, the adopted worldview continued to have various effects on the way the state was run, through politics, economics and the social sciences. Eventually the Scientific Revolution lead to an unprecedented wealth of knowledge in the seventeenth and eighteenth centuries, which culminated in the Cartesian and Newtonian worldview; a 'world as a machine' view that successfully described nature's goings-on by a series of deterministic and atomistic formulae.

The objective method preached by Descartes and the phenomenal success of the Newtonian physics deeply impacted on Western society at large, and fitted well for an Industrial Age that was maturing by the end of the eighteenth century. In turn, the industrialized society exulted and encouraged all ideas that went in the direction of added mechanization. The 'soft sciences' followed the models of the 'hard sciences' and, little by little, man-as-a-machine grew further and further from Mother Nature. The nineteenth century, the golden age of the steam engine, brought forth new concepts born in the study of thermodynamics: *entropy* described a universe-machine that was running down irreversibly. Yet it was still a machine.

The heroic years of the Modern period were as many years spent in the search of a (over)simplification of man's life, to the detriment of nature. Man was left behind staring at a meaningless void; pessimism was in the air, and for all the excitement it instigated in the world of science, Einstein's Relativity theory could not but dig the gap between man and nature deeper and deeper. The two World Wars came as the ultimate symbols of the destructive power of science, and perhaps nothing is as expressive of the worldview/ sciences link as the Cold War years that followed.

Ours has been an age of alienation, and many authors converge on finding the roots of this *malaise* in the worldview brought about by 'Newton's bleak vision':

> The immutable laws of history portrayed by Marx, Darwin's blind evolutionary struggle and the tempestuous forces of Freud's dark psyche all, to some extent, owe their inspiration to Newtonian physical theory. All, together with the architecture of Le Corbusier and the whole vast array of technological paraphernalia that touched every aspect of our daily lives, have so deeply permeated our consciousness that each and every one of us sees himself reflected in the mirror of Newtonian physics.[1]

From anti-war movements to grass-roots ecological parties, a strong anti-scientism has swept over the last decades of the twentieth century, advocating a return to nature and the adoption of sustainable lifestyles. In parallel there has been a resurgence of spirituality in many forms, from New Age cults to religious fanaticism. The cultural crisis is severe and more or less universal, yet there seems to be a way out. Fritjof Capra, author of *The Tao of Physics*, wrote in 1982, a decade before the realization of the global Internet:

[this crisis] derives from the fact that we are trying to apply the concepts of an outdated worldview – the mechanistic worldview – to a reality that can no longer be understood in terms of these concepts. We live today in a globally interconnected world, in which biological, psychological, social, and environmental phenomena are all interdependent. To describe this world appropriately we need an ecological perspective which the Cartesian worldview does not offer.

He further insists:

What we need, then, is a new 'paradigm' – a new vision of reality; a fundamental change in our thoughts, perceptions, and values. The beginnings of this change, of the shift from the mechanistic to the holistic view of reality, are already visible in all fields and are likely to dominate the present decade.[2]

At the same time, Nobel laureate Ilya Prigogine was proposing precisely that. In his excellent *Order out of Chaos* (1984) he writes:

The human race is in a period of transition. Science is likely to play an important role at this moment of demographic explosion. It is therefore more important than ever to keep open the channels of communication between science and society. The present development of Western science has taken it outside the cultural environment of the seventeenth century, in which it was born. We believe that science today carries a universal message that is more acceptable to different cultural traditions. [...] a message that concerns the interaction of man and nature as well as of man and man.[3]

Science seems to have almost come full circle. It is putting its hand out towards society and the soft sciences, trying to bring back together man and his environment. Similarly, society should embrace this new attitude, and the soft sciences should meet the hard sciences half way in a techno-spiritual and ecological worldview. Such a worldview will be described in the coming chapters. But first, let us follow the major developments of science that have brought us thus far.

The organic worldview

From antiquity to the sixteenth century, most civilizations adopted what can be considered an 'organic' worldview:

'People lived in small, cohesive communities, and experienced nature in terms of organic relationships, characterized by the interdependence of spiritual and material phenomena, and the subordination of individual needs to those of the community.'[4]

The 'official' worldview of the Middle Ages was based on a scientific framework outlined by Thomas Aquinas when he merged Aristotle's philosophy of nature with Christian Theology and Ethics. The resulting worldview was the fruit of a science interested in the *meaning* and purpose of things, rather than in their functioning and control. The spiritual values that overlaid the science of the period produced what would be called today an 'ecological' worldview, where nature was looked upon as a 'nurturing mother', not a mere object to control:

> The image of the earth as a living organism and nurturing mother served as the cultural constraint restricting the actions of human beings. One does not readily slay a mother, dig into her entrails for gold, or mutilate her body ... As long as the earth was considered to be alive and sensitive, it could be considered a breach of human ethical behavior to carry out destructive acts against it.[5]

This ecological paradigm allowed man to live in harmony with his environment, in a culture that respected the very sanctity of Mother Nature. Unfortunately this paradigm was shaken away radically in the sixteenth and the seventeenth centuries, when the sanctity of science, the 'official' worldview of the Church, was given a series of destabilizing blows at the hands of renowned philosophers. (The term 'philosophy', from the Middle Ages to the nineteenth century, was used in a very broad sense that included what we now call 'science'.) This set about what historians refer to as the Age of the Scientific Revolution, whose greatest actors were Copernicus, Galileo, Descartes and Newton.

The Scientific Revolution

In 1543, the astronomer Nicolas Copernicus introduced a courageous hypothesis. His 'heliocentric view' placed the sun at the

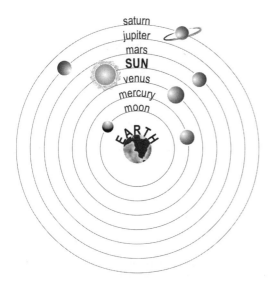

Figure 2.1
*The geocentric model with the Earth fixed at the centre
of the universe.*

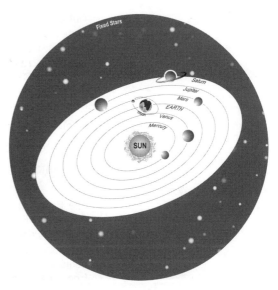

Figure 2.2
*The heliocentric worldview shifted Earth to an orbit around
the sun.*

centre of the universe, and relegated Earth to the subordinate position
of an orbiting planet. This hypothesis clashed with the thousand-year-
old geocentric dogma of Ptolemeus and the Bible (Figure 2.1), and it
was not until Galileo pointed the newly invented telescope to the skies
in 1609 and analysed planetary motions in physical terms that the old
cosmology was overthrown and the Copernican hypothesis proven as
scientific fact. Earth was not central to the scheme of things anymore.
The first punch had been thrown (Figure 2.2).

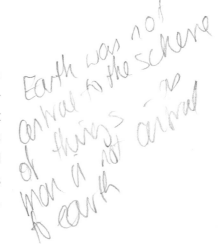

However, Galileo's role in the Scientific Revolution goes far beyond this
episode. He devised a methodology that would be applied with
phenomenal success throughout modern science: the formulation of
the laws of nature through the language of mathematics, based on
experimental observation. Noting that mathematics could only describe
quantifiable properties, he postulated that scientists should confine
themselves to the study of the shapes, the numbers and the
movements of matter, while colour, sound, taste, smell, and all 'subjective mental projections' should be excluded from the realm of scientific enquiry.

v. important

proxd

> Out go sight, sound, taste, touch and smell and along with them has since gone esthetics and ethical sensibility, values, quality, form, all feelings, motives, intentions, soul, consciousness, spirit. Experience as such is cast out of the realms of scientific discourse.[6]

Henceforth a wedge was cast between the body and the soul, as, parallel to Galileo in Italy, Francis Bacon was busy in England formulating the empirical method of science and the inductive procedure of experimentation.

> The Baconian spirit profoundly changed the nature and purpose of scientific quest. From the time of the ancients, the goals of science had been wisdom, understanding the natural order, and living in harmony with it ... the basic attitude of scientists was ecological. [...] in the seventeenth century this attitude changed into its polar opposite, from yin to yang [...]; from integration to self assertion. Since Bacon, the goal of science has been knowledge that can be used to dominate and control nature, and today both science and technology are used predominantly for purposes that are profoundly antiecological.[7]

Not only that, but the very terms Bacon used to express his new experimental methods verged on the sadistic: Nature had to be 'hounded in her wanderings', 'bound into service', and 'made a slave', as her secrets were 'tortured from her'.[7] This phenomenal contrast with the earlier paradigm of nature as a nurturing mother was to develop further into the Scientific Revolution, replacing the organic worldview with a mechanistic vision. The major paradigm shift that was to shape so much of the further development of Western civilization was to be sealed by the work of two brilliant men of the seventeenth century, Descartes and Newton.

The Cartesian schism

At the young age of 23, René Descartes (Figure 2.3), considered today as the father of modern philosophy, set about building a new scientific method. Influenced by the new physics and astrology, he completely rejected all traditional knowledge. Bertrand Russell saw in this a 'fresh attitude, unseen since Plato, a sign of a new self confidence, that resulted from the progress of science'.[7] Virtually single-handedly, Descartes sowed the seeds of an entirely new worldview. The

Figure 2.3
René Descartes (1596–1650): 'All science is certain, evident knowledge.

Cartesian paradigm was grounded on the firm belief in the certainty of scientific knowledge. 'All science is certain, evident knowledge', he confidently declares in his *Discourse on Method*, and here, 'at the very outset', according to Capra, 'is where Descartes went wrong': relativity and quantum theories were to show us 300 hundred years later that scientific truth could be *relative and uncertain*. Yet this Cartesian 'scientism' continues to shape Western society today.

Descartes, a mathematician and philosopher, applied analytical methods that broke up any thoughts and problems into small bits and solved them as separate pieces. This was his most profound contribution to modern science. A truly effective method that has led us to the moon, this has also had a tremendously negative side effect: our blind respect of the Cartesian method has led us to fragment our education, and hence our minds, into atomistic little boxes through which we hope to comprehend the complexity of the world. In his foreword to *Order out of Chaos*, Alvin Toffler insists:

> One of the most developed skills in contemporary Western civilization is dissection: the split-up of problems into their smallest possible components. We are good at it. So good, we often forget to put the pieces back together again. ... in this way, we can ignore the complex interactions between our problems and the rest of the universe.[8]

Descartes' approach, being based on a mathematical method, echoed Galileo's. Here again, Descartes' search for a complete and certain natural science advocated a total separation between objective and subjective matter, even in the biological realm. The *res cogitans* (mind, the 'thinking thing') and the *res extensa* (matter, the 'extended thing'), were two fundamentally separate realms, and had no interconnections whatsoever except perhaps a common creator: God. But like all fine subtleties, even this was ignored in the further development of the scientific worldview. The material universe as now envisioned was little more than a machine without life, meaning or spirituality. It was in such a worldview that Newton was to set about formulating his laws of physics.

Newton's mechanism

Descartes had only managed to set about a theoretical mechanical framework. It was Isaac Newton (Figure 2.4), in the last quarter of the seventeenth century, who was to give practical form to the Cartesian vision by developing a complete mathematical formulation of the mechanistic view of nature, thus achieving a grand synthesis of the ideas of Copernicus, Bacon, Galileo and Descartes. Newton's genius devised the exact mathematical formulae (he invented calculus for the occasion) determining the movement of all objects, from stones to planets, and this is what made them so important: they were applicable *universally*, and correctly fitted observation of natural elements. Undeniably, the universe in the Newtonian vision was as Descartes

Figure 2.4
Sir Isaac Newton (1642–1727): 'absolute, true, and mathematical time, of itself and by its own nature, flows uniformly, without regard to anything external'.

imagined; one immense mechanical system, following exact mathematical laws, and those laws were attainable through our mere reason.

Beyond proving the validity of the Cartesian mind/matter schism, Newton's laws had another significant effect on the worldview. The Newtonian universe not only functioned as a machine, it also functioned in an absolute space, equal in all directions and similar in all points; an empty three-dimensional space, a 'neutral container' completely independent from the phenomena inhabiting it. Furthermore, these phenomena were described in an absolute time, also a neutral background: 'absolute, true, and mathematical time, of itself and by its own nature, flows uniformly, without regard to anything external', postulates Newton himself in his *Principia* (*The Mathematical Principles of Natural Philosophy*, 1687). The Newtonian paradigm thus emphasized a qualitative time/space schism that could only add to the determinism and the absolutism of the modern vision. God built the machine and set it to work at the beginning of time, and since the world continues on a deterministic causal path towards the future, there was the gist: the state of a system at any time in the future could be predicted with absolute certainty, based on the detailed description of its state at any anterior moment.

The Newtonian physics and the Cartesian method were to be so successful in the coming century that other disciplines started to emulate their approach. Chemistry was one of the first, and thus many chemical phenomena were successfully interpreted as the interaction of Newtonian particles: John Dalton devised a mechanical model of the physical behaviour of gases, the 'atomic hypothesis', assuming all chemical elements to be made up of atoms obeying Newtonian laws. This was the first step to the unification between chemistry and physics, and the first in a series of examples of other sciences turning to physics for methodology.

Descartes himself, who had suggested a mechanistic approach to physics, astronomy, biology, psychology and medicine, had already expressed this vision. The eighteenth century – the Age of Enlightenment – was to extend this approach to the social sciences:

anthropology and sociology. One of the most prominent contemporaries of Newton was the philosopher John Locke (1632–1704), who attempted an atomistic study of human society; just as Dalton reduced the properties of gases to the motion of their atoms, so Locke reduced social patterns to the behaviour of individuals. He believed that human society was governed by deterministic natural laws in a similar fashion to the Newtonian world-machine. This concept was to have tremendous repercussions on the further development of classical psychology, spawning behaviourism and Freudian psychoanalysis.

Locke's ideas also outlined the role of government as that of an 'easer' of natural laws, including freedom and equality of all individuals in a society, and the right to property. These in turn became highly influential concepts in the development of the modern framework of politics and economy, and soon took form in, for instance, the American Declaration of Independence, and were concretized in the Constitution of the USA. What was clearly happening was a mutual affirmation and confirmation between the ideas of physics, the worldview this described, and those of most socio-political and cultural disciplines. Yet Newtonian physics were to be challenged by new discoveries in the nineteenth century.

Entropy versus evolution

Newtonian laws were universal and described phenomena that happened in an absolute, and *reversible*, time. The keyword here is 'reversible': Newton's formulae functioned accurately in both directions, independently of the direction of time. Research on the steam engine produced new theories and formulae that did not: thermodynamics introduced the concept of *entropy*, or the measure of a system's disorder. Thermodynamics showed that many systems tended towards states of greater probability, i.e. states of less order. Such systems were *irreversible*. For example, if a puff of smoke is let into a room, it will dilute evenly into the air, and not congregate into one corner. If left to itself, it will never take back its initial position. A teapot falls to the ground and shatters to a thousand pieces. Newtonian physics can describe its movement as it falls and the movement of each piece flying away, according to accurate laws. These laws work similarly if the pieces came together again and made up a teapot that lifted itself up back on the table, but such a thing does not happen in real life. Entropy adds an *arrow* to time. This concept from the Second Law of Thermodynamics*, while representing one of the most important discoveries of nineteenth century physics, could not be accounted for by Newtonian formulae.

Another school of thought was to evolve from the new ideas of change, growth and development in time: *evolutionism*. It spawned evolutionary theories of the solar system by Kant and Laplace, and evolutionary political concepts by Hegel and Engels. Its epitomical formulation was Darwin's theory of the evolution of species, based on Lamark's *coup de force* decades earlier. Lamark had done the unthinkable: he 'turned the ladder of explanation upside down', proposing that life started with the tiniest amoebas and ended up in man, the total opposite of the Biblical hierarchy where man is created first, after the angels, but before the rest of the animal kingdom. The biological theory of evolution proposed a world where systems moved towards higher organization and complexity – higher order. In that, it was running counter to physics' evolutionism, where systems moved towards increased disorder. The link between the two was to be found in statistical theory, stating that systems *could* tend towards order but that that was highly unlikely. It was only when Boltzmann introduced the notion of *probability* into the picture that thermodynamics grounded itself on a sound Newtonian base: simple closed systems permitted reversibility, but once these systems became more complex and made up of great numbers of molecules, reversibility became highly improbable, while the increase of entropy became virtual certainty. In a closed isolated system with a large number of elements, entropy will inevitably increase to a state of maximum disorder, bringing the system to its 'heat death'. In classical physics, the whole universe is facing such a fate: the great clockwork is inevitably grinding towards a halt one day. Open systems, on the other hand, more easily develop order and complexity.

*The first and one of the most fundamental laws of physics, 'the law of *conservation* of energy' states that although energy in a closed system can change form, its total sum is always conserved throughout the process. The Second Law of Thermodynamics is the 'law of *dissipation* of energy' and states that whilst the *total* energy is conserved, the *usable* energy (mechanical energy) gets dissipated into heat, friction, and so on, and cannot be reused with 100% efficiency. Hence, the 'arrow of time', and the ineffable increase in entropy, or disorder.

These conceptions are considered today to be at the roots of modern chaos and complexity theories, which are coming close to accurate descriptions of a living universe. But most importantly, and in direct relevance to our theme, these discoveries showed the first limitations of Newtonian physics, and laid bare the over-simplifications of the Cartesian worldview. Yet Newtonian physics would continue to be considered correct and accurate until the early years of the twentieth century, when one man alone, an obscure patent office clerk in Vienna, was to revolutionize the whole world of physics with two masterly concepts. In 1905 Albert Einstein single-handedly constructed the theory of relativity, and sowed the first seeds of what was to become, two decades later, quantum theory.

Einstein's revolution

Newtonian physics, as we saw in the previous paragraph, were showing limitations in their description of the world. Their 'universality' was being questioned by the discoveries in the world of thermodynamics and electrodynamics. In particular, physicists were trying to explain radioactivity and X-rays, the behaviour and nature of light, and the relationships between the four known forces of nature (the electromagnetic force, the strong nuclear force, the weak nuclear force, and the gravitational force) … to no tangible success.

Enter Albert Einstein. This young genius applied a completely fresh approach to dealing with physics, publishing in 1905 his revolutionary *Special Theory of Relativity*, and another article on electromagnetic radiation, which would develop to become the seed of quantum theory during the following decades. His search for a unified foundation to physics, through the language of geometry and mathematics, led him to reintroduce the concept so cherished by nineteenth century mystics: the Fourth dimension*. Only Einstein's feat was that, instead of a fourth *spatial* dimension, he defined *time* to be the fourth dimension of our universe. For the first time in the modern history of science he unified Space and Time into the space–time continuum, and from that deceitfully simple change of viewpoint was able to unify energy and matter,

*For a detailed and fascinating account of the Fourth dimension and current theories of multi-dimensional universes, read Kaku.[9]

then light and gravity, into a simple formula, $E = mc^2$, with some of the farthest reaching implications ever conceived thus far.

> ... the essence behind the theory of special relativity, [...] is that time is the fourth dimension and that the laws of nature are simplified and unified in higher dimensions. Introducing time as the fourth dimension overthrew the concept of [absolute] time dating all the way back to Aristotle.[10]

The relevance of this feat to our subject at this point is that he had suddenly demolished one of the most entrenched concepts of the Newtonian worldview: the absolute space and the absolute time were now relative and dialectically linked as *space–time*. Time flowed at different rates depending on where and when it was measured. Furthermore, Einstein's unified formulae showed that energy and matter were one, or at least that energy could be created from matter and *vice versa*. This of course explains the A-bomb amongst other things, but it also meant that matter and energy were, just like space and time, unified into a new concept: *energy–matter*.

Einstein did not stop there, and went on to find the relationship between these two new concepts, finally making another revolutionary discovery: gravity (energy) was no more than an illusion caused by the curvature of space–time due to the presence of heavy objects (matter such as planets). The *General Theory of Relativity* of 1915 sealed the reputation of Einstein as the greatest physicist that ever lived. In it he showed that space–time was not a simple flat Euclidian geometry, but had a complex curved and interactive geometry that could be described by a special type of mathematics that a fellow called Riemann had developed a few decades earlier as a purely theoretical exercise.

The whole concept of gravity was revolutionized: instead of a force between two objects as in Newtonian physics, gravity was now seen as a bending of space–time by any large object. Any other mass in the vicinity of the first one also bends space–time, and together they move in that deformed environment (Figure 2.5). Even light was thus bent by mass; in reality a ray of light

Figure 2.5
According to relativity, gravity is an illusion caused by the warping of space–time by the presence of large mass or energy. Space–time bends like a rubber sheet when you place a weight on it.

would only be following the shortest route from its source to our eyes. In a flat Euclidian space that would be a straight line, but in curved space–time it would be a curve. Consequent experiments proved this to be correct. In particular, in 1919 a British expedition to West Africa, led by A. S. Eddington, was able during a solar eclipse to measure the slight shift in the apparent position of stars due to the mass of the sun. The result made Einstein himself an overnight star: for weeks, newspapers and magazines ran articles on the man and his strange ideas; it was the beginning of his myth-like fame, and a plethora of artistic and literary references to relativity were to follow.

The effect of the theory of relativity on the worldview was paralleled with new ideas in the arts and some of the soft sciences, history, and anthropology (literature, cubism, surrealism, the revival of relativism all crisscrossed the strange world of relativity, according to Friedman and Donley's remarkable *Einstein as Myth and Muse*[11]). It was fairly clear that the Newtonian worldview was shaking, and that change was in the spirit of the time. Einstein became the emblem of that change. It is not very probable that Lenin knew of Einstein's work when he called, in his *Materialism and Empiro-Criticism* (1908), for a *new dialectic* between matter and energy: 'No longer could they be viewed as separate entities, as Newton had done. They must now be viewed as two poles of a dialectical unity. A new conservation principle was needed.'[12] Yet it is remarkable that the work of both men, both imbued with the spirit of change that was in the air, would coincide in time. Einstein's discovery of the inherent power of the atom and his subsequent letter to Roosevelt in 1939 explaining the potential feasibility of an atomic bomb, and Lenin's establishment of the Soviet Union, were indirect ingredients in the psychological, social and geo-economic forces that shaped the world during the Cold War*.

Einstein's stature as the 'good genius' has loomed high in the popular and official imagination of the past century (Figure 2.6), crowned by his selection as 'Person of the Century' by *Times* magazine (31 December, 1999). The Theory of Relativity gave the cultural world a fresh attitude 'wary of "common sense" based on too limited an experience in the cosmos; [it showed] that two observers might describe the events of the world differently, and yet (barring blunders) each might be correct'.[11] In parallel to its actual physical conceptual changes, many misconceptions were spread through the populariza-tion of the theory – in particular, some claimed that

*Einstein's work, particularly the theory of Relativity, was not the 'key to the atomic bomb' as historical misconceptions claim; it was rather his stature as a public figure of genius that made his letter to Roosevelt a key element in the American pursuit of the bomb. It is reported that when FDR read that Einstein believed a bomb could be based on atomic energy, and that the Nazis could be developing one, he ordered immediate action, which came in the form of the Manhattan Project, under which the first atomic bomb was designed. Einstein himself had nothing to do with that project as a physicist. A detailed history of the development of the bomb and Einstein's role in those years, in addition to a fascinating account of relativity-inspired literature is found in Friedman and Donley's *Einstein as Myth and Muse*.[13]

Figure 2.6
The world's most recognizable scientist, and his most celebrated formula ... here seen on the cover of a caricature magazine from Iran (courtesy Javad Alizadeh, Tanz-o-Caricature, Tehran, Iran. http://www.tanz-o-caricature.8m.com/)

relativity theory meant 'everything is relative', and that it gave up determinism and objectivity.

Einstein resented these misconceptions; after all, he was a stark classicist when it came to the belief in objective deterministic science. However, the public was so taken by his image that any revolutionary new idea in science seemed to be naturally attributable to him.

In the 1920s, nuclear physicists found incredible phenomena at work at the heart of matter. These phenomena were so unexpected, so revolutionary, that most scientists, including the great man himself, refused to accept their implications on science. Those who did dare question these implications developed quantum theory.

3
quantum theory:
an introduction to basics

It is often stated that of all the theories proposed in this century, the silliest is quantum theory. In fact, some say that the only thing quantum theory has going for it is that it is unquestionably correct.[1]

When the history of the [twentieth] century is written, we shall see that political events – in spite of their immense cost in human lives and money – will not be the most influential events. Instead the main event will be the first human contact with the invisible quantum world and the subsequent biological and computer revolutions.[2]

What then, makes the new physics so unusual in its description of our world that the great Einstein himself could not comprehend it? It is simply its counter-intuitiveness. Yet as Michio Kaku reminds us, 'scientific revolutions, almost by definition, defy common sense',[3] and quantum theory does indeed defy all we have been used to so far, to the point that quantum scientists themselves still have trouble understanding what their formulae *mean* exactly. It is remarkable that quantum theory is still referred to as 'the new physics', even though it was first articulated in the early twentieth century. This is because of its relative youth compared to 'classical physics' – in other words Newtonian science, which has shaped our worldview for the last three centuries. Quantum theory was so revolutionary in terms of both process and meaning of the world that it necessitated a radical change in the concepts of space and time, matter and energy, subject, object and causality. It came as such a shock to scientists that although they solved its mathematical equations quite early, it took them decades to come to grips with what it all meant. Meanwhile it had explained almost everything that needed to be explained in the physical world, and permitted such amazing technological feats as the laser, television, and digital computers. In fact, it is physics' most successful and most accurate theory ever.

So how are we going to understand what quantum physics is, if nuclear scientists themselves couldn't! There is no need to panic. We do not need to understand how it all works; all we need is to know about its main conceptual framework and how it differs from the classical framework. Because we are looking for the effect of such a new set of concepts on the world-view, we do not have to worry about the exact scientific source of those concepts. In all cases they are based on different popularizations of quantum theory through the literature of either quantum physicists themselves or popular science writers.

In other words, we will not have to deal with scientific or mathematical formulae; simply with ideas and concepts. We will wonder about philosophical implications, some of which will remain speculative. Yet the mere fact that such questions are raised by the new ideas is by itself fascinating. A quick overview of the major concepts of the quantum theory will be followed by a formulation of what a 'quantum' worldview looks like. This presentation will form the basis for the conceptual and metaphoric language developed in the rest of the book to consider the Quantum City. So brace yourself, and let us hop into the jumping universe!

Searching for the light

It all started with light, just like the Genesis in the Bible. The history of light is a fascinating journey that started millennia ago with the ancient Greeks, passing by the Arab Empire, up to quantum theory. It is told in captivating detail in John Gribbin's books, *In Search of Schrödinger's Cat*[4] and *Schrödinger's Kittens*.[5] The relevance to our theme is how the tug-o-war between the two main views of light as particles or as waves in the last few centuries came to be solved by quantum theory, as it adopted the radical both/and notion of parti-cle~wave duality.

Newton insisted that light was made up of little parti-cles, for the predictable reason that his universal laws were so successful when applied to particles, and he naturally wished them to include the behaviour of light. During the same period, experimental observations started pointing to an interpretation of light as a wave: Grimaldi (1618–1663) and then Euler (1707–1783) published theories interpreting the effect of diffraction as a wave behaviour not explainable by the Newtonian corpuscular theory. However, it was not until Fresnel (1788–1827) and Poisson (1781–1840) that the nature of light was finally settled to be wave-like. Michael Faraday (1791–1867) then developed the idea of electromagnetic force fields and showed that light behaved just like an electromagnetic wave. Finally, James Clerk Maxwell (1831–1879), after inventing colour photography in 1861, produced his master-piece in 1864; the four equations that carry his name and describe all electromagnetic behaviour – including that of light waves.

So by the end of the nineteenth century, light was firmly established to be a wave, and no one dared go back to the particle theory. However, Max Planck's (1858–1947) work on radiation introduced the idea of quanta in 1900, and Einstein himself grabbed the concept in 1905 to explain the photoelectric effect as a result of light being quantized – in other words, of light behaving like packets, or particles. By 1915, Milikan had shown that the light quanta were real and physical, not just mathematical tricks. Planck (1918), Einstein (1921) and Milikan (1923) all received the Nobel Prize for their work, and in 1926 the name 'photon', from the Greek *photos* (light) was given to the quanta of light. Studying the strange behaviour of photons gave birth to quantum physics.

Classroom physics 101: the two-hole experiment

Easily the most recurrent story in accounts of the history and nature of quantum physics is the seemingly benign 'two-slit experiment' or 'the experiment with the two holes'. But, as anyone would tell you, 'the more you know about the experiment with two holes, the more mysterious it seems'.[6]

The experiment requires a simple set-up: a light source and a receiving wall or screen, between which is placed an opaque board with two narrow holes in it. When the light shines through both holes, a pattern of light and dark bands appears on the screen (Figure 3.1). This is a pretty straightforward effect recognized as a typical wave interference pattern. The two holes act as two sources of light

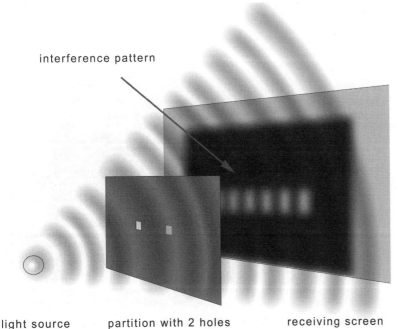

interference pattern

light source   partition with 2 holes   receiving screen

Figure 3.1
The two-hole experiment; when both holes are open, a wave interference pattern appears on the screen.

waves. When two waves meet, they mathematically combine to create an interference wave. The peaks and valleys of the waves add up to create light bands, or cancel each other out to leave dark shadow bands. This is exactly what we expect and see when we know that light behaves as a wave as it passes through the two holes in our experiment, so not much mystery so far – light is a *wave*.

If we close one of the holes, the resulting pattern is a single light spot aligned with the hole and the light source (Figure 3.2). Not much mystery here either, there is only one source and the light wave doesn't interfere with anything. Now let us vary the experiment by making the light source shoot out one photon at a time (this has already been done many times since the 1980s), with still one of the holes closed. If the receiving screen is photo-sensitive (can be marked by light, like photographic paper for example), each photon will leave a tiny dot on it. Because the hole is much bigger than a photon, a multitude of photons hitting the screen in sequence will not be exactly coincident with one another, but will create a slightly larger spot – a distribution pattern. This is exactly the same as if the light source was

Figure 3.2
When one hole is open, there is no interference.

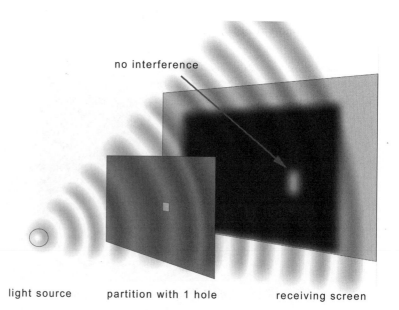

light source   partition with 1 hole   receiving screen

sending out continuous light through one hole as at the beginning of the experiment. The distribution pattern would be similar if we scaled up the experiment and shot bullets through one hole onto a wooden screen. Photons and waves coming through one open hole do not create interference patterns, neither do bullets.

All right, one more time: let us open the other hole for the bullets, and continue shooting randomly, one bullet at a time, in the general direction of the board. The receiving screen will record two distribution patterns, one behind each hole, exactly similar to the distribution we would get if we closed one hole for half the time and the other for the rest of the time we were shooting. Nothing exciting here; bullets, because they are classical particles, do not interfere with one another and therefore will never create an interference pattern, regardless of the number of holes open.

Let us now shrink the experiment and go back to tiny holes, both open, a photosensitive receiving screen, and a photon gun, capable of shooting one particle of light at a time in the general direction of the screen. Because the two holes are open, each photon going through the board has a 50-50 chance to pass in either one of the holes, on its way to

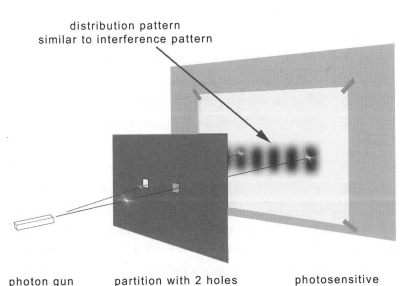

distribution pattern
similar to interference pattern

photon gun   partition with 2 holes   photosensitive
paper

Figure 3.3

Even if we fire light particles (photons) one at a time, each one seems to 'know' whether both holes are open or not. When both holes are open, the successive photons distribute themselves into an interference pattern similar to that of the waves from Figure 3.1.

leaving its mark on the photosensitive screen. Common sense tells us that the final pattern on the screen should be similar to the bullets through two holes distribution pattern, since every photon did its journey from the photon gun to the screen by itself. Each photon was not shot before the previous one entered through one of the holes and hit the screen, and therefore each shot is like an independent experiment of its own. Yet, against all commonsense expectations, the resulting pattern is exactly similar to the wave interference pattern of the first experiment: the distribution pattern of single photons going through two holes is an interference pattern! (Figure 3.3.)

How could that have happened? 'Although each photon starts out as a particle, and arrives as a particle, it seems to have gone through both holes at once, interfered with itself, and worked out just where to place itself [on the screen] to make its own minute contribution to the overall interference pattern.'[6] Why does the same photon act differently whether one hole is open or both? How could a single photon *know* the second hole is open at the moment it goes through one of the holes? How can it interfere with itself, *as if it was going through both holes at the same time?*

It gets worse: light is not the only element that has this insane property. The two-hole experiment has been repeated in the 1980s using electrons instead of photons, and in the 1990s using atoms, which are 22 million times more massive than electrons. In both cases the behaviour of these elements, largely considered as particles, was similar to that of the photons: they started out and landed as particles, but travelled as waves, going through both holes at the same time and interfering with themselves. Where do these weird characteristics begin and end? At what scale can we start shooting a bullet through a hole without worrying that it might go through two holes at the same time? These are some of the questions that have troubled physicists since the 1930s. They led to the formulation of the quantum theory, which has turned physicists' conception of space, time, causality and objectivity upside down. In fact it has reshaped their whole notion of reality, and the following new concepts are at the roots of this drastic change.

The particle~wave duality: the Principle of Complementarity, or the both/and logic

Possibly the most revolutionary and definitely the most important concept of quantum theory is the *particle~wave duality* of all matter. Particle and wave are both classical concepts that were clearly defined and followed their own laws in Newtonian physics. Particles, as discrete space-limited objects, followed the Newtonian mechanical laws, while waves, as deformations in an underlying medium (such as ripples on a water surface or electromagnetic vibrations in the air) followed a different set of laws. Both sets of laws are sound, accurate systems that correctly predict the behaviour of particles on one hand, and of waves on another. The search for the nature of light showed behaviours that fell into both patterns at the same time, and forced quantum physicists to redefine their concepts to accommodate the unexpected nature of the subatomic world.

According to quantum theory, the behaviour of all subatomic matter can be consistently described as solid particles or as waves; microscopic billiard balls or overlapping undulations or probability waves in a mathematical space. All matter is *both* particle-like *and* wave-like. Bohr's Principle of Complementarity postulates that the two descriptions complement each other; choosing one description over the other yields incomplete results: 'a whole picture emerges only from the "package deal". Like the right and left hemispheres of the brain, each description supplies a kind of information that the other lacks'.[6] This of course was not the case in Newtonian physics, where elementary particles were thought of as tiny atoms that would bump into, attract or repel each other, according to preset deterministic predictable rules. Particles had preset places in time and in space. Waves – such as light waves or sound waves – were thought of as vibrations in a background medium and covered whole regions of time and of space simultaneously. Only waves were secondary and not considered as 'matter', which was consistently made up of solid particles.

The nature of the wave in the particle~wave duality is subtly different from the waves we are used to observing in the physical world, such as waves on the water surface after we drop a pebble in a pond. According to the 'Copenhagen Interpretation' of quantum theory (to which we shall return in the coming pages), the waves are in fact mathematical probability waves that calculate *the possibility of the presence of the particle* at different points in space. The bizarre thing is that even though these are not 'real material' waves in the classic sense, they do have a very real and very physical effect on reality, and therefore they have to be taken into consideration in the experiments. In fact, those probability waves permeate all time and space, to the point that every quantum particle does interact with every other quantum particle through its probability wave. While the mathematics of probability waves are similar to those of 'traditional' waves, the calculations involved are extremely complex; however, they do yield equally phenomenal accuracy, and the wave aspect is thus inseparable from the particle aspect of matter.

The Principle of Complementarity as defined by Niels Bohr links opposite representations of the same object, stating that it is impossible to know all about an object by looking at only one of the two complementary aspects.

> Bohr's principle of complementarity asserts that there exist complementary properties of the same object of knowledge, one of which if known will exclude knowledge of the other. We may therefore describe an object like an electron in ways which are mutually exclusive ... without logical contradiction provided we also realize that the experimental arrangements that determine these descriptions are similarly mutually exclusive. Which experiment – and hence which description one chooses – is purely a matter of human choice.[7]

The new concept of the duality of matter itself is in sharp contrast to the mind/body schism of the Cartesian worldview. If we think of mind as a collection of thoughts, memories, feelings, beliefs, and all the subjective intangible aspects of ourselves, it is easy to see how it can be compared to the wave aspect of matter – while the physical being is best described as a particle limited in time and space. Cartesian either/or dualism is replaced by the both/and logic of the particle~wave duality. Moreover, many authors and even physicists themselves, such as David Bohm, Danah Zohar or Michio Kaku, saw in that a clear parallel with the Chinese concept of Yin/Yang comple-mentarity, while others such as Zukav[8] thought probability waves were similar to the organic energy fields strongly present in ancient organic worldviews. That can only hint at the philosophical implications of such seemingly straightforward principles. These implications will be tackled in the coming pages; meanwhile, our foray into the strange quantum universe must continue.

A jumping universe: random leaps beyond space and time

The word 'quantum' comes from the Latin *quanta*, or discrete quantity, that in physics came to describe the finite units of energy at play in the subatomic world. Planck was the first to discover that energy was radiated discontinuously, as 'packets', and Einstein would later call these *quanta* – hence the term quantum mechanics. Niels Bohr subse-quently showed that subatomic particles could only exist at certain levels of energy and not between such levels. An electron orbiting a nucleus would *jump* from one level of energy to another, depending on the number of *quanta* of energy absorbed or given off from it.

This meant that motion is not continuous as we are used to perceiv-ing it, but rather proceeds in minute jumps – quantum leaps that defy our idea of time and space. In addition, jumps could cover more than one step, leaping ahead in so many whole quanta, and that, accord-ing to quantum theory, can happen for no apparent cause whatsoever and totally randomly. What's more, the electron sometimes seems to jump to all possible states *simultaneously*, checking its possibilities in what is termed *virtual transitions* (represented by the wave function), before 'choosing' a particular state to rest in. Similarly, all quantum particles transcend time and space and gain holistic, non-local proper-ties.

The extraordinary image that clashes most with the Newtonian deter-minist physics is the randomness of it all – in other words, the lack of any clear causal law to the state changes. Quantum particles are jerky, moody little things that change state for no apparent reason: 'the best we can do is give the probability of a jump. The smallest wheels of the great clockwork, the atoms, do not obey deterministic laws.'[9] Even more extraordinarily, they can jump to places Newtonian physics simply do not allow them to go – like through opaque walls! The probability of a jump is in fact the probability of the particle being at one location or the other. In between the different states or locations, reality is nothing more – *and nothing less!* – than an infinity of possibilities, calculated by a mathematical probability distribution wave. The effect known as 'quantum tunnelling', which is at the heart of most of our contemporary electronic technology, permits an electron to jump out of a hermetic container and reappear just outside it. This is because the probability wave that governs its behaviour gives it a minute chance of being outside, and the electron sometimes jumps on that chance. It gets better: because the probability wave is a mathematical rather than a physical wave, it is not limited by space and can actually have a non-zero value at any point in the universe; claiming that any point in space has a zero probability value would be deterministic, and that would clash with the Principle of Uncertainty. This simple fact means that an electron has a minute, but *non-zero*, chance of disappearing from its container and reappearing at the other end of the universe instantaneously ... and yes, you guessed it, there is a tiny, but non-zero, chance for all the atoms that make up your body to disappear and reappear on Mars!* But while you are still here, let us discuss another major tenet of quantum theory, which I am sure you have heard of before.

*Not to worry though, the probability of this happening is really so minute it would take many times the age of our universe for it to happen!

The Uncertainty Principle: does God play dice?

God does not play dice!
(A. Einstein)

Einstein, stop telling God what to do!
(N. Bohr)

Heisenberg's Uncertainty Principle, much like Einstein's relativity theory, is one of the most quoted concepts in non-scientific literature.

'Uncertainty' is certainly a buzzword these days, and that is great, but few understand what indeterminacy means in the quantum world, or where it comes from. After a year trying to figure out if an electron was a particle or a wave, Niels Bohr and Warner Heisenberg, two of the fountainheads of quantum theory in the 1930s, went their separate ways and each came back with his own interpretation of what ruled the experimental results. Bohr discovered the Principle of Complementarity, while Heisenberg came back with an essentially equivalent idea, but regulated through a mathematical formula. Heisenberg's Uncertainty Principle regulates the Principle of Complementarity by stating that the accuracy of measurement of either complementary aspect is inversely proportional to the other. In other words, it is impossible to measure both complementary aspects precisely. For example, an accurate measurement of the position of a particle will totally blur all information about its momentum (its direction and speed), and inversely, an accurate measurement of its momentum will totally blur all information about its position – if we know where a particle is we cannot know where it is going, and if we know where it is going there is no way of knowing where it is!

This was another blow for classic determinism, which required a precise knowledge of the state of a system at a point in time to calculate its state in a future time. Suddenly, physics cannot predict events with accuracy anymore, it can only calculate the probability of them happening. 'At the subatomic level, matter does not exist with certainty at definite places, but rather shows "tendencies to exist", and atomic events do not occur with certainty at definite times and in definite ways, but rather show "tendencies to occur".'[10] These tendencies are calculated using statistical mathematics, and are represented by the 'wave function' associated with each particle. Probability has a large role in the events of the subatomic world, much to the opposition of the Newtonian deterministic or the Cartesian rational worldview. Even Einstein could not accept this concept, famously interjecting: 'I cannot believe that God plays dice with the Universe!' and declaring quantum theory as incomplete. In fact that aspect of the theory was only one of the problems posed to positivist scientists such as Einstein, who strongly believed in the objectivity of science and the intelligibility of the universe through physics. The Principle of Complementarity and the Uncertainty Principle were to constitute the core of what became known as the Copenhagen Interpretation of quantum theory.

The Copenhagen Interpretation: WYSIWYLF

> If a tree falls in the woods and there is nobody there to see it, did a tree really fall in the woods?
>
> (Zen proverb)

The Copenhagen Interpretation of quantum theory, named after the Danish physicist Niels Bohr, is one of the suggested explanations for the paradox of Complementarity. The two-hole experiment showed a direct relationship between the observer (or the method of measurement) and the observed result: if you look for a wave you get a wave, but if you look for a particle you get a particle – a sort of 'What You See Is What You Look For' situation; physicists doubted the very *reality* of their findings.

The Copenhagen Interpretation accepts the results of the experiments by admitting the demise of strict determinism and objectivity and replacing them by a statistically based reality – a reality of probabilities – and an interactive rather than an absolute universe, dependent on how an observer chooses to observe it. It holds up the excellent internal consistency of the theory as a potent enough proof of its validity, without the need to worry about whether what it said of the universe was commonsensical or not. This interpretation, also known as the standard interpretation of quantum theory, does not really explain how the wave function collapses into reality; only that it does when a conscious observer looks at it. In other words, reality is a blur unless observed. Taken literally, this asks the question, who observes the observer so that his wave function collapses into the 'real' person he is? If it is the world outside the observer, then who observes the world to collapse its wave function? Eventually, the whole universe needs an observer outside it to make it real, or requires a circular relationship between all observers and all observed phenomena!

The importance of indeterminacy to the dual aspect of matter destroyed the classical notion of solid objects at the heart of matter. The solid material objects of classical physics are replaced by wave-like probability patterns. In such a world, where an electron *might* be a wave, or *might* be a particle, where anything and everything *might* happen, only predictable through the probabilities of the *wave function*, when – or why – does the wave function collapse into a tangible reality? – or in Zohar's words, 'where the essential basis of reality as we know it consists just of so many possibilities, how can anything in this world *ever* become actual, or fixed?'.[11] The Copenhagen Interpretation answers this dilemma by stating that the real world is a mental construct shared by its different observers: the wave function collapses when and how it is looked at; the world exists only when it is observed. In a sense, by asking which came first, mind or matter, quantum theory has induced a mind–matter unity of deep philosophical implications.

Complementarity stated that quantum particles such as electrons are neither a wave nor a particle, but something else we cannot fathom with our classical language. When observed it will show us one or the other of those aspects, like opposite sides on the same coin. Exactly what the coin itself is, is treated in the pragmatist tradition: it is not possible to form a vision of truth outside of our direct sensory experience of it, and hence trying is futile.

> The extraordinary importance of the Copenhagen Interpretation lies in the fact that for the first time, scientists attempting to formulate a consistent physics were forced by their own findings to acknowledge that a complete understanding of reality lies beyond the capabilities of rational thought. ... The new physics was based not upon 'absolute truth', but upon *us*.[12]

The standard interpretation thus solves the practical problems of the theory but avoids answering the philosophical implications that it raises. In fact, the immense experimental and practical success of the theory meant most physicists were very happy using it without thinking about existential matters, with the notable exception of Einstein, of course. Erwin Schrödinger, who initially introduced the concept of wave function, devised a 'thought experiment' to prove the absurdity of the

Copenhagen Interpretation, but his cat-in-the-box paradox has been popularized in the last 60 years more to support than to refute the insanity of quantum theory. The following is a simplified account of the experiment, and it is introduced here as an example of the conceptual implications of the observer–observed relationship.

Imagine a hermetic, opaque box large enough to fit a cat and a device with a special mechanism. The device is triggered by a random atomic event that has a 50-50 chance of happening – for example, atom decay of a known particle (never mind the technical details). When activated, the device drops either food or poisonous gas into the box, with equal probability (Figure 3.4). We place a small healthy cat in the box, which is then sealed closed (allowing for air for the cat of course), and we press a button to trigger the 'diabolic' device. Unless we look inside the box, we cannot know what has happened, whether the cat got food or poison gas. All we can say with absolute certainty is that, after we pressed the button, there was a 50 per cent chance of the cat being alive and well, and a 50 per cent chance of it being dead – nothing weird in classical logic. But since the device is based on an atomic, and therefore a quantum, event the formalism of the quantum theory obliges us to consider the device to be 'smeared' in a super-position of states that will only split once we open the box and look inside. The 'wave function' that describes the state of the atomic device, and therefore of the cat itself, holds both possibilities and will collapse into either reality – dead cat or live cat – only once we observe it. Until we open the box and peek inside, the cat is neither alive nor dead, it is *both!*

Schrödinger devised this thought experiment to raise the issue of scale, and to show the absurdity of applying quantum theory to large-scale, tangible objects. But the paradox that it raises: 'how can a cat be dead and alive at the same time?' is at the heart of quantum theory's bewildering concepts, and does get a few physicists and philosophers to claim that the 'dead cat' or 'live cat' does not take on an objective existence until somebody actually looks at it. In a way it is equivalent to the famous Zen question of the tree falling in the woods. Whatever the reality of the situation, the mere fact that the question is raised in

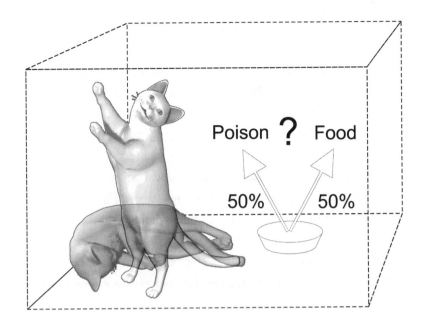

Figure 3.4
Schrödinger's quantum cat is 'dead–alive' until we open the box and check on it.

science is a revolution in itself and a major departure from the three centuries since the Age of Enlightenment.

Non-locality and relational holism: the universe is one

Schrödinger's cat is not the only thought experiment devised to bash quantum theory. Einstein, as a staunch opponent of quantum theory, spared no expense in trying to disprove it, mostly through a challenging correspondence with Niels Bohr, who always found some flaw in Einstein's reasoning that would salvage the theory. But one of the most fantastic attacks came in the form of a thought experiment, devised with the help of Podolsky and Rosen in 1935, known as the E–P–R paradox. We will not go into the complicated details of the experiment, but the crux of it is as follows.

We start with a two-particle system of zero spin. This is a quantum system made up of two correlated particles with complementary properties. For example, if we are measuring the spin* of the particles, if one is spinning up, the other has to be spinning down, and if one is spinning left, the other is definitely spinning right. If quantum

*The spin property of subatomic particles is not exactly the same as the spin of a small ball, but for the point at hand it is sufficient to think about it as such.

theory is correct, even if we separate the two particles by immense distances, the correlation holds. The E–P–R thought experiment imagined such a situation where the two particles were each sent to one end of the universe, without carrying any observation on either. In other words, we do not know what spin either of them has; all we know is that whatever spin states they are in, those spin states are complementary and correlated. To simplify matters, let us consider that the initial system only allowed for up/down spins. The spin state of each particle is represented by the wave function that gives each particle a 50 per cent chance, say, of being in the up state, and a 50 per cent chance of being in the down state. Whatever state the first particle is in, the second is in the other state, but we cannot know which (up or down) until we observe the spin of one or the other of the particles.

According to quantum theory, the moment we observe one of the particles its wave function collapses into one of the states possible – for example, its spin is measured to be 'up'. At the same moment, because the two particles are correlated, the wave function of the other particle also collapses, and we can safely say that it has a spin of 'down' without even needing to observe it directly. What this implies is that there has been a non-local violation of causality: 'something' told the second particle what to do *instantly*, as if it were continuously and immediately aware of what was happening at the other end of the universe without any link with its quantum twin particle. The keyword here is 'instantly', as it means that the 'something' was not transmitted through any physical means (such as an electromagnetic effect, or a force, or even light) since those would be bounded, according to relativity theory, by the speed of light. Any signal travelling at the fastest speed known to man, the speed of light (300 000 km/s), would take *hundreds of billions of years* to cross such a distance. The 'instantaneity' of the collapse means a supra-luminal message has been sent – a message faster than the speed of light. The correlation is independent from its locality in space–time. When Einstein came up with this thought experiment, he thought it would prove quantum theory wrong precisely because it would break local causality.

Physicists spent the next 50 years trying to express the thought experiment into a testable, practical experiment. In the early 1980s, Alain Aspect in Paris finally performed the experiment with photons ... and it proved beyond the shadow of a doubt that non-locality did occur. Against common sense, against relativity theory, and against Einstein's disbelief in what he called 'spooky action at a distance' (unfortunately he wasn't alive anymore), quantum theory passed the test once more.

Non-locality is probably the 'spookiest' prediction of quantum theory. It deals the final blow to everything we thought we knew of the way space and time functioned. By the end of the twenti-eth century serious research was hoping to use this property of correlated matter to develop, amongst other things, a working version of the Star Trek 'beam me up' teleportation machines, another potential technological revolution based on quantum theory. Before we discuss how all the unexpected properties of the subatomic world came to shape a different paradigm, we need to introduce two final but extremely impor-tant concepts: quantum field theory and quantum vacuum fluctu-ations.

Multidimensional quantum field theory: malleable energy patterns

We have encountered, very briefly, Faraday's electromagnetic force fields in the discussion on the nature of light. We have also seen how Einstein unified mass and energy and defined gravity as a warping of space–time, thus defining the gravitational force field. Quantum physicists in turn developed quantum field theory in the 1940s (QED, quantum electrodynamics) to describe the life of subatomic particles, which were only 'visible' through their interactions with each other and with the experimental appara-tus. Complex but straightforward mathematical functions describe the state of the field at any moment in time. Each point in the field is represented by a sequence of numbers that give all the properties of that point. Because the interactions are very real, almost more 'real' than the particles, the field is considered to be the actual physical reality of the world. Heinz Pagels[13] lists the five central dogmas of relativistic quantum field theory:

1. The essential material reality is a set of fields.

2. The fields obey the principles of special relativity and quantum theory.

3. The intensity of a field at a point gives the probability of finding its associated quanta – the fundamental particles that are observed by experimentalists.

4. The fields interact and imply interactions of their associated quanta. These interactions are mediated by quanta themselves.

5. There isn't anything else.

Throughout the twentieth century, physicists developed field theories for each of the four forces of nature: gravity, the electromagnetic force (electric and magnetic fields), the 'weak' force (responsible for radioactive decay), and the 'strong' force (holds quarks together). In the 1970s, they realized that all the forces except gravity were unified at higher energies, and could be described within a single field theory. A couple of decades later, they found that a model of the universe with ten dimensions (rather than the usual four dimensions of space–time) could have 'enough room' for the unification of all the forces including gravity.[1]

Meanwhile, quantum theory had shown that all particles could be thought of or described as the quanta of the different fields, and that the intensity of the field at any point in space–time would give the probability of finding a particle at that point. When the Uncertainty Principle is applied to the field concept, amazing things start to happen.

The vibrant vacuum: something out of nothing

Quantum field theory says that each point in the field is a potential particle, which materializes once the intensity of the force at that point passes a crucial quantized level. One must imagine an 'existence barrier', like a malleable nylon cover stretched over the surface of a pool, with potential particles swimming under the surface (Figure 3.5). When energized, the potential particles gather speed and try to jump out of the water, and into existence. They only become 'real' if their momentum is high enough to break the nylon cover and reach out into the air. If one looks closely, every square millimetre of the cover is alive with an infinity of little waves and bulges, as potential particles jump up and 'bump their heads' on the cover without breaking it. According to quantum theory, reality is a whole ocean of potentiality, a vacuum that is far from being a sterile void. The fluctuations of the vacuum are ruled by the Uncertainty Principle, the principle of energy conservation, and the energy–matter equivalence.

The Uncertainty Principle, as you recall, states that the certainty of the knowledge of the energy level of a particle is inversely proportional to the certainty of the knowledge of its position in space–time (the certainty of its momentum is inversely proportional to that of its position). Therefore, the uncertainty of the energy of a potential particle over a tiny moment in time is

Figure 3.5
The potential pool: whenever a virtual particle (or event) breaches the existence barrier and 'jumps' into reality, it becomes an 'actual event'. The probability wave describes the chance of this happening at every point of the pool.

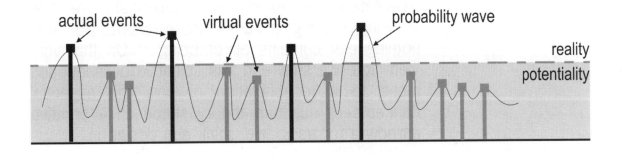

infinite. Over a long moment in time the uncertainties cancel out, but for extremely short instants we cannot claim with total certainty that the energy level is *not* high enough. This means the energy of the quantum field at that point might reach the critical level necessary for the actualization of a potential particle into a 'real' particle. Some of the swimming particles randomly reach enough momentum to break through the nylon cover, and into existence.

The principle of energy conservation requires the total energy of the system to remain constant, so an actualized quantum in fact comes in the form of a particle/anti-particle pair (complementary elements of equal but opposite energy levels, e.g. an electron/positron pair) that re-annihilates into oblivion as soon as it comes into existence. This coming into existence of something out of nothing, in fact of matter out of energy and back, is of course unheard of in classical physics, yet the effect has been observed many times in experiment. Every creation and annihilation of those virtual quanta is a quantum fluctuation of the vacuum. Physicists believe the universe was created by a similar but gigantic fluctuation of the vacuum: the Big Bang. The Big Bang theory expresses most awesomely the quantum concept of 'something out of nothing', but also links everything in the universe together into a common initial identity. In fact it is equivalent to the idea of 'everything out of potentiality': 'Theoretical and experimental physicists are now studying nothing at all – the vacuum. But that nothingness contains all of being'.[14] On this very 'Zen' note we shall end this scientific overview and move to a recapitulation of how the essential concepts of quantum theory shape an alternative paradigm for us to live, think and design in.

interlude:

mathematical chaos and urban complexity

A tractal pattern

The twentieth century saw the birth of many more 'revolutionary' scientific discoveries, from systems theory and cybernetics to fractal and chaos theories; complexity and information theory to Grand Unified Theories and string theory. Yet I have consciously limited the scope of the first, historical, part of this book up to quantum theory. The reason is simple. I believe the quantum revolution was a qualitative jump that was necessary for the further development of these theories. The conceptual and practical consequences of quantum theory allowed the birth of these ideas. The most straightforward example is the development of powerful computers that eventually allowed the discovery of the fractal world, as fractal geometry requires incredibly tedious iterative calculations.

Since the early 1950s a new metaphor has been circulating in the world of mathematics, and it started to permeate the arts and architecture very strongly in the 1980s and the first half of the 1990s: chaos and complexity theory and the world of fractals.

Developed by Polish-born mathematician Benoit Mandelbrot over a period of 30 years, fractal geometry has come to signify the *geometry of chaos*. What at first might seem a contradiction in terms is in fact based on the discovery that even the most seemingly chaotic of effects that are observed daily in nature hide a deep underlying order of almost perfect beauty.

"The key insight ... revolves around the idea that the world is chaotic, discontinuous, irregular in its superficial physical form but that beneath this first impression lies an order that has been simplified away in terms of the continuous and the smooth in all previous attempts at scientific understanding."[1]

Chaos and fractals have been of great help in the solution of mathematical complexity problems and, combined with catastrophe theory, even in modelling – with catastrophe theory and thanks to supercomputers – the behaviour of economy, politics and the weather, and even linguistics.

More recent research focuses on the application of fractal geometry and analysis to architecture, design and, eventually, cities. Batty and Longleys' excellent book *Fractal Cities* provides a sweeping overview of the theories and produces fine examples of fractal urbanization. Their contention is that 'much of our pre-existing urban theory is a theory of the fractal city'[1], and thus fractal geometry holds a key tool for the analysis and simulation of the growth of the city.

The subject is too rich and too important to attempt a simplification here. I strongly urge the interested reader to delve into the fascinating world of fractals and natural geometry through the works of Batty and Longley[1], Mandelbrot[2], (1983), Bovill (1996), and James Gleick's now classic *Chaos: the Birth of a New Science*[4].

The key point of relevance to our subject is the fact that while the science of fractals does produce forms that are recurrent in nature and proposes a theory that has universal applications, with connotations of wholeness, infinite scalability or indeterminism (at least of the impracticality of determinism), it remains too objective and too formal a science – in my opinion – to be able to deal by itself with the totality of the urban realm. It cannot completely account for the *subjective* aspects of the urban realm due to the inherent need of coherence between the mind of the human users and the form and meaning of their artefacts, but it could be quite useful as a *tool* for simulation and analysis of urban form.

In all cases, fractals, chaos and complexity theories are inherent components of the new world-view that we have chosen to name 'quantum' because quantum theory is its most charismatic player. The alternative language this book suggests or extends is, therefore, based on the current paradigm heralded by relativity, quantum theory and the new sciences of chaos and complexity and their interaction with practical life.

Many authors in many various disciplines have undertaken a similar task lately. Chris Abel's enriching collection of essays *Architecture and Identity*[5] provides sweeping links between architecture and the different 'new sciences' of the twentieth century (remarkably, with barely a mention of quantum theory). Meanwhile, Manuel de Landa's highly original *A Thousand Years of Nonlinear History*[6] uses complexity theory to address, amongst other things, human settlements and the development of European geo-economy.

Nørretranders' splendid *The User Illusion*[7] gives some of the most thought-provoking ideas about self-organization and fractal dimensions as related to human products and consciousness. Zohar and Marshall's inspired and inspiring *Quantum Society*[8] was a revelation to me, while Charles Jencks' *Architecture of the Jumping Universe*[9] left my intuition that the 'new' paradigm could not but affect our philosophies, attitudes, and hence our environment unquenched.

Jencks chose slightly *exagéré* formal interpretations and implications, and the overall tone sounded more like a quick overview of trendy designers' works than the more generic approach the present book adopts. For example, I strongly disagree with his interpretation of the 'wave aspect' through a literal formal motif of 'wavy lines'. *Architecture of a Jumping Universe* remains nonetheless a good account of the changing interests of architecture in resonance with scientific paradigms.

In terms of content, then, Jencks' interests are more formal and aesthetic, while those of this book are spatial and inter-relational. Behind this difference lies the *nuance* that differentiates between fractal geometry and quantum theory. While there are overlaps between the two areas of research and what some see as an 'off the wall' quality to the idea of adapting them to urban design, their consequences are possibly different, at least because their subject matter is different, but they are most probably complementary. Well used they should lead to an alternative – and better – practice of design in general and urban design in particular.

You will find that Chapter 4, The Quantum Worldview, and the subsequent analysis of the quantum city, are not 'pure'. The quantum metaphor is strongly contaminated by concepts from complexity, chaos, information theory, self-organization concepts, systems theory, and so on. This is not merely because, in my opinion, most of these ideas were direct or indirect offspring of the conceptual and practical innovations of quantum physics, but also because I feel my own conceptual mindset is strongly permeated by all these ideas. It is difficult for me to distinguish between the influences of the different theories I have encountered since I first 'tilted' on quantum theory. It is just as difficult to segregate between the different memories and experiences that make up one's culture or persona, so why should one want to do so in the first place?

4
the quantum **worldview**

le 21 siècle sera spirituel ou ne sera pas.*
(André Malraux)

Art does not evolve by itself, the ideas of people change
and with them their whole mode of expression.
(Pablo Picasso)

The twenty-first century will be spiritual or it will not be.*

Quantum theory came as a shock to the scientific community. The extraordinary image of reality it exposed was as unsettling as Copernicus kicking Earth out of the centre of the universe four centuries before, and it took physicists decades to come to terms with what it meant. Even now many still haven't accepted the philosophical and existential questions it raised, and prefer to concentrate on what can be done with it, not what it does to the worldview.

There are at least two worldviews associated with any particular knowledge revolution: the official worldview and the popular worldview. The official worldview is the model Authority uses to describe the universe. Authority can be political, religious or scientific, or a combination of those aspects. The popular worldview is the root metaphor people collectively form through the dissemination of the official worldview. For millennia both official and popular worldviews coincided, but as scientific knowledge expanded, the scientific authority developed worldviews more and more at odds with the political and religious official views. As popular knowledge in turn expanded, so did the power of scientific authority grow more and more independent. Political authority finally decided to stand by the scientific rather than the religious paradigm, as the popular worldview gathered momentum in that direction, and religious power in the Western world lost ground just in time to allow the scientific revolution to sweep over the old continent. Scientific objectivism quickly permeated the social, economical and even artistic disciplines, riding on the success of Cartesian rationalism and Newtonian determinism. The lifestyle changes brought about by the ensuing industrial revolution further freed the populace from the official worldview, until the larger-than-life character of Einstein recaptured the scientific and the political, as well as the intellectual and popular, imagination.

The worldview revolution brought about by relativity theory in the aftermath of the Great War of 1914–1918 was widely embraced by a Western world embittered by the massive destruction brought by the machines, but hopeful of a new world order triggered by the fall of the Austro-Hungarian and the Ottoman Empires. The first three decades of the twentieth century represent an impressive moment in the history of the post-mechanical worldview. Einstein developed relativity, Bohr and Heisenberg developed quantum theory, James Joyce published *Ulysses*, and T. S. Eliot wrote *The Waste Land.* Marcel Duchamp painted his *Nude Descending a Staircase*, and Picasso developed cubism. Scientists became philosophers, and philosophers became scientists. Einstein himself, Arthur Stanley Eddington, Henri Bergson, Bertrand Russell and Alfred North Whitehead, to name but a few, all mulled over the existential implications of the new physics. During the coming decades, with the development of radio, cinema, television, the A-bomb ... science created both the media and the story.

By the time the scientific authority came to grips with its own discoveries at the end of the 1920s, the world was undergoing an economic crash that was soon followed by a political one. The Second World War plunged the world in turmoil again. Six years and two atom bombs later, people were again disenchanted by the scientists, who were left to their own devices to poke deeper and deeper into the quantum world. The politicians had found a new world-view with which to control the masses. The politics of the Cold War had enough subject matter to keep the press and the media running. Even the race into space was sold as a race between the two superpowers. However, it bought the scientists new gadgets and particle colliders with which to test their ideas, and allowed them to develop the fantastic technologies that have shaped our generation's worldview. From the laser to the digital computer, the Internet and portable telephones, we have come to realize a need for complexity and connectedness that echoes the language of modern physics.

The paradigm shift that struck the scientific community in the 1920s had been acknowledged by Lewis Mumford as early as 1934 in his *Technics and Civilization*,[1] and a decade later by Siegfried Giedion in his *Mechanization Takes Command*.[2] But it wasn't until the last few decades of the twentieth century that the 'quantum wake' started to propagate, as numerous authors from different disciplines began to announce the winds of change that were building up into a major paradigm shift. While popular science books never stopped selling, in the 1970s and early 1980s many philosopher-physicists such as Fritjof Capra, Gary Zukav or David Bohm picked up on the coincidence between the language of quantum theory and Eastern philosophy, bringing the new physics to a New Age audience and away from 'mainstream' literature. By the mid-1980s, new theories of consciousness based on quantum chemical models of the brain (some of which first appeared in scientific literature as early as 1970) triggered a plethora of more 'serious' quantum-related publications, taking the quantum worldview well into the politically correct 1990s, where it found itself related to social and ecological theories.[3,4] Meanwhile art and literature have had the time to play around with the different concepts, from the four-dimensional space–time field of cubist paintings, the 'everything is relative' miscon-struction of postmodern art, or the psychedelic digital images of fractals and complexity theory. In a very similar way to the forces that brought about the move into the Cartesian and then the mechanical worldviews of the previ-ous centuries, lifestyle changes due to new technologies, new ideas mediated by the arts and humanities and popularized by books, television and the Internet have built up towards a new worldview that promises a renewed communion with nature through science.

An ecological vision without the paranoid anti-scientism of 1960s ideologies is at hand. As we enter the third millen-nium, the ideas that have been tossed at us over the last century have matured into a sober worldview that allows for a relational metaphor to carry our complementary ideas and formalisms. Cinema, literature and the arts have long been experimenting with the new ideas. Neurology, psychology, sociology, economics and business management, to name but a few disciplines, have already developed convincing models based on the quantum paradigm.

Urban studies, and more specifically architecture, were much slower than the rest of the arts to pick up on the new worldview. In fact, many accuse modernism of being the last child of the mechanical paradigm,[3] deep into the twentieth century. This delay could be related to the conservative nature of educational institutions,[5] but is probably due as well to the generation or two it takes for those already adapted to a new worldview to come to decision-making positions, capable of influencing architecture and the city. Whichever the case, the required quarantine period is over, and the quantum paradigm is finally making its mark on the physical urban realm.

In the coming chapters, we shall try to define an urbanism largely imbued with the quantum worldview. That worldview is the child of a century of percolation of science into both the intellectual and the popular imaginations. It cannot claim any scientific exactitude: it grows around a selective association of meanings derived from a collection of themes that have appeared in science books, popular literature, the media, television shows, cinema and the Internet over the last few decades. Rich with insights, but also with misconceptions, this new paradigm blurs the boundaries between relativity, quantum theory, complexity and chaos theories, current cosmology, Eastern philosophy, New Age 'mysticism', and whatever resonates with the wishful optimism of our generation. I have found some common themes to be more relevant to life in the quantum city than others. They help to create a mindset with which I believe urban design will be approached in the twenty-first century.

Dynamic contextualism

Space and time are relative, not absolute, realms. They affect and are affected by observation and action. Space and time are interconnected into a relativistic field called space–time. Time itself as a dimension is as important as space in the description of any reality. The concept of *contextualism* is at work in the space–time continuum, meaning any fixed set of variables and rules will inevitably lose its certainty as time passes and locations change, however minute the change: the quantum worldview is inherently indeterminist, and its indeterminism springs from the fact that it is dynamic, ever-changing in both space–time (quantity) and meaning (quality).

Relational holism

Man, nature and the universe are one in the sense that their interactions have mutual effects on each other, and it is impossible to reduce the whole to any of its constituent parts. Interconnections and interactions sometimes transcend time and space, causing effects and reactions in the most unexpected of ways. That is why it is not possible to predict accurately the future of any exact situation involving complex systems, but only to work out its *probability patterns*. The new worldview is probabilistic and holistic.

Meaning and spirit

Everything has a dual aspect: from a stone to a tree to the human being, or complex artefacts, it is impossible to pin down and define anything without considering *both* its objective and its subjective aspects (see Table 4.1). While the objective aspect might deal with physical material form, quantity and composition, the subjective aspect can consist of different *inherent* qualities, or result from the interactions and interconnections between them. As the whole is more than the quantitative sum of its parts, it can take on additional, emergent qualities. These could range

Mental	Physical
subjective (private)	objective (public)
non-spatial	spatial
qualitative	quantitative
purposive	mechanical
possessing memory	no memory
holistic	atomistic
emergent	composition
intentional	'blind'; non-intentional

Table 4.1
The mental and the physical
(Source: Zohar[3])

from socio-cultural and philosophical interpretations (meaning, symbolism, community, memory, identity ...) to practical and functional ones (function, activity, sustainability, sociability, economy ...). The quantum paradigm gives back *meaning* to the material world: it is also spiritual.

Table 4.2

The quantum view of the world as a set of dualities

EITHER/OR: dualism		AND/BOTH: duality
particle	wave	particle~wave duality
Newtonian physics	relativity	quantum physics
architecture	planning	urban design
mechanical	organic	
'thingy-ness'	'relating-ness'	
building	function	
user	community	
individual	society	
solo	team/group	
physical space	cognitive space	
quantity	quality	
function	art	
left brain	right brain	
space	time	
design by foresight	design by hindsight	
utopia	retrotopia	
modern	postmodern/deconstruction	'quantum city'
postmodern pastiche	critical regionalism	
'Man' first	'Nature' first	
determinism	acausal nihilism	
private	public	
objectivity	subjectivity	
analysis	intuition	
linear	random	
local	global	
form	meaning	
mechanical	spiritual/purposive	
body	soul	
physical	mental	
res extensa	res cogita	res publica
urbs	civitas	city

Tolerance and pluralism

The uncertainty and the complementarity principles can be extended as analogies to different fields and disciplines. When applied to inquisitive research it immediately appears that the either/or logic cannot but be reductive. Quantum theory replaces the either/or logic of the classic worldview with a both/and approach that permits the co-existence and accepts the complementarity of opposing values (see Table 4.2). It transcends Cartesian *polar dualism* into what we can call *complementary duality*. It promises a worldview where the inner and the outer realms are united again, but also a world where diversity, hybridity and heterogeneity can be creatively active in the production of a positive whole. It is not a worldview where anything and everything is valid, but where a conjunction of things can emerge as a valid and meaningful whole. The quantum worldview is tolerant and pluralistic.

Technology and ecology

Quantum physics has given the twentieth century most of its life-changing practical technology. From television and lasers to microchips and the Internet, everything we seem to depend on since the electronic revolution relies on quantum theory to function. Unlike the science that preceded it, the technologies associated with the quantum world seem more constructive than destructive: the tanks of the mechanical age, or the nuclear bombs (wrongly) associated with relativity theory, have been replaced by DNA, the science of life, and the Internet – the world-wide web of knowledge. Science is not as scary anymore. The anti-scientism that had opposed the Cold War and the mushroom-induced flower power that opposed the atomic mushroom have become less virulent. With alternative technologies as an option for a better world, the overall drive of science itself seems much more ecological. Electronic microscopes probing the sub-atomic world are looking for the origins of life, while digital images from the Hubble space telescope search for the origins of the universe. Thanks to its notions of interweavability of the whole universe, from the infinitely large to the infinitely small, and the recognition of the human as intrinsic to nature, the quantum worldview is as technological as it is ecological.

The main concepts behind quantum theory thus describe a world of relationships, overlaps of space and time, of tangible matter and ethereal, almost abstract wave patterns – a world of systems of dualities where nothing is perfectly deterministic, and where nature regains its unpredictability. Most importantly, it is an ecological worldview, in its description of a mutually creative relationship between the observer and the observed in the quantum realm.

Science has come full circle. If we embrace what it is telling us, our civilizations might finally regain the 'organic' worldview described by Prigogine and Stengers as 'characterized by the interdependence of spiritual and material phenomena'.[6] But this statement remains a 'New Age' advice typical of millennium expectations, until we effectively find practical applications to it that are firmly grounded in scientific fact.

Recent research (by Penrose, Bohm, Zohar and Marshall) looks for the answer in the role of human consciousness* and provides solid evidence of quantum laws at work at the level of neurons and synapses in the brain, convincingly building a quantum mechanistic model of consciousness and of psychology. Zohar and Marshall succeed, in *The Quantum Society*,[4] in producing a quantum model of sociological behaviour. If such research proves to be correct, then it is only logical that the products of the human mind might be modelable according to quantum laws. This book proposes to extend this logic to include one of man's largest products: the city. If the city itself is not modelable, due to its scale, then the *conceptual language* inherent in those laws should at least allow us to sketch the modus operandi of a quantum city.

*Some even entertain an age old idea of *panpsychism*, where even inanimate matter – including electrons – possesses a very basic form of decision-making properties, or consciousness.[7,8]

interlude:

feng shui
or the tao of the city

Urban space has always been influenced by the world-view of its users. Before the scientific revolution, that worldview was the result of a traditional set of beliefs that still echo in some contemporary non-Western civilizations.

Ancient Egyptian, Roman and Greek cities were laid out in relation to astrology, the position of the planets, or the path of the sun. The Celts positioned their temples, houses and settlements according to invisible subterranean force fields, or what they called 'telluric fields'. Ancient Asians and Native Americans planned their settlements according to geomancy, a science based on the symbolism and powers of the geographic context and natural landscape elements.

While these civilizations are long gone, some of their beliefs have transgressed time and continue to influence modern-day decision-making, from personal superstitions to actual planning policy. In particular, the millenary Chinese philosophy of feng shui continues to inform architecture and planning in modern-day China and Hong Kong, and any construction project in those countries requires a feng shui consultant to pass it.

Recent research has defined a clear interpretation of feng shui beliefs into urban design rules that, interestingly, can be tweaked to agree with some of the most parochial Western planning techniques.[1] The importance of such a philosophy as feng shui is that it is strongly rooted in the culture and worldview of the Chinese people- in other words, it permits urban design to produce environments that 'make sense' to their users through a set of values and meanings that are timeless. Its goal is to reunite humanity and nature.

In fact, Chinese philosophy believes that man emerged 'from the bowels of the Earth like any mountain or plant, and therefore was one of them in spirit'.[2] This permitted the Chinese to develop much exquisite art and landscape, and lively and living cities – at least until Communism in mainland China and capitalism in Hong Kong inadvertently disturbed this harmony.

While Dr James Lovelock's famous Gaïa hypothesis[3] proposes that humanity and all other living systems are symbiotically correlated into a super-organism that is the living planet Earth, thus agreeing with the ancient Chinese beliefs, Fritjof Capra, in his intriguing *The Tao of Physics*[4], explores the philosophical parallels between quantum theory and Chinese Taoism.

In a similar fashion, in *The Turbulent Mirror*[5] F. D. Peat probes the relationship between chaos theory and ancient Chinese cosmologies and philosophy. The same author then found similar links between quantum physics and American Indian worldviews, in his fascinating *Blackfoot Physics*[6]...

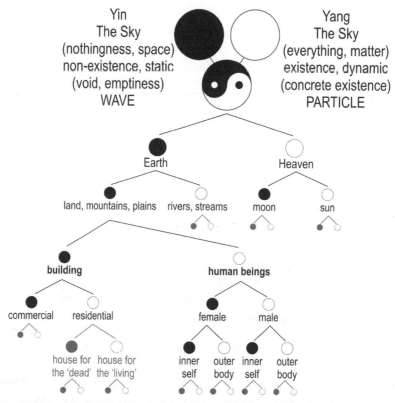

The dualities of Yin/Yang. It is interesting to note the 'building~human beings' duality at the centre of the tree.

The quantum worldview and the Chinese worldview are related through this 'ecological' belief, the correlation between man and nature and the importance of change (Confucianism) and equilibrium (Taoism) together in the harmony of the world. Through the concept of yin/yang (see figure left) and of particle~wave dualities, both Chinese Taoism and quantum theory describe the world as a dialogue of inseparable complementary opposites.

Feng shui requires the knowledge of a set of laws varying from cosmology to topographical symbolism and social interaction. It shares interesting similarities with some concepts of the quantum worldview:

- The *chi* life-force: the 'wave aspect' and its event horizon (see figure below)

- The cycle of changes, and Confucian philosophy: indeterminism, dynamism, contextualism

- The *Tao*, or 'the way' of harmony and balance: order/chaos equilibrium

- *Ren He*, defined as 'people's relationship with each other and to their surrounding environment'[1]: quantum society, and the observer/observed dialogue.

Chinese philosophy thus uses feng shui as a set of rules and superstitions to shape a relevant physical environment. If modern physics is to Western culture what feng shui is to Eastern culture, then

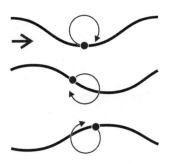

The Motion of Good Chi.

the quantum metaphor might provide a framework for an urban design strongly rooted in a shared set of philosophical and scientific beliefs that might transcend Western culture, and work as a translation interface between both complementary civilizations.

5
20th century
cities

Industrialization and modernist urbanism: the mechanical worldview takes physical form

The incredible advances in science and technology during the nineteenth century resonated with political and economical theories, bringing about profound changes in lifestyles and modes of production. Breaking almost totally with traditional frameworks, industrialization made the individual the core unit of society, as opposed to the family-unit of agrarian structures that had endured for more than five millennia.

> Rather than attaching rights and prerogatives to particular groups and persons, or being guided by custom or tradition, modern institutions tend to be governed and guided by general rules and regulations that derive their legitimacy from the methods and findings of science.

The scientific revolution started a major population explosion, as death rates dropped with new health-related knowledge, and industrialization brought with it an unprecedented boom in urbanization, exponentially raising the density of cities and requiring new ways of dealing with the population. While extensive analysis and critique of the effect of industrialization and the new methods of production on urban space has been published in the last decades, our concern here is to understand the direct link between the worldview of the moment and urban space.

The twin-headed worldview built around Newtonian mechanism and Darwinian evolutionism eventually expressed itself in the first half of the twentieth century through the dichotomy between the modernists and the ecologists. The former, represented by icon figures such as Le Corbusier and Mies Van der Rohe, virulently attacked all tradition past and called for an embrace of the industrial *Zeitgeist* as a paradigm for all human production.

Although this is a reductive reading of the modernist agenda, it is easy to recognize the affinities between the 'world as a machine' vision of Newton, the 'city as a machine' of the industrial age, and the 'building as a machine' of Le Corbusier, who in his 1923 *Vers une Architecture* called for the embrace of machine production and aesthetics as the correct expression for modern man. Using an almost Platonic discourse, Le Corbusier advocated an urban landscape of atomized yet repetitive buildings, each a machine to live in (Figure 5.1).

> It is a spectacle organized by an architecture that uses plastic resources for the modulation of forms seen in light. A city made for speed is made for man.[2]

Even as some of his discourse seemed informed by Einstein's newly published work on the speed of light, Le Corbusier's fanatical positivism totally adhered to

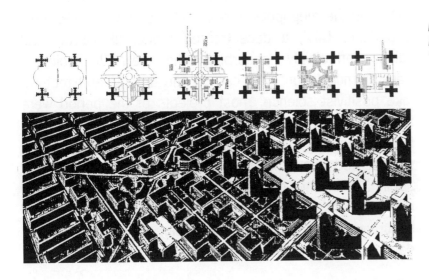

Figure 5.1
Le Corbusier's vision of a 'contemporary city'.[2]

the Newtonian mechanistic worldview. Functionalism, or the total segregation of all the functions of the city into zones (administrative, cultural, educational, residential and so on) is a typical result of the industrial reductionist project, itself the direct descendant of the Newtonian/Cartesian approaches.

The 'International Style' advocated by the Modern Movement can thus be read as a consequence of man's independence from nature and context, from time and space, and the superiority of his intellect that has so successfully found the underlying universal laws that govern all nature.

Ecologists, in contrast, 'instinctively turned away from modern architecture in the new garden cities and elsewhere, for primarily they were concerned with the human element to be found in the familiarity and gentleness of traditional homes, gardens and trees'.[3] They preferred to ignore modern technology totally and instead advocated a return to car-free environments starting from the same viewpoint of anti-density ... While Le Corbusier radically thought to raze Paris to the ground to provide a sterile *tabula rasa* for his *Ville Radieuse* model, whose rules were coded in the 1933 Athens Charter, Frank Lloyd Wright expected the megapolis to decline,[4] proposing in 1935 his 'Broadacre City', a decentralized model utopia of rural values effectively absorbing the new technologies (telecommunications, the car ...) and organic architecture. Like positivist science, most projects of the period were fascinating in their formalism, sometimes graphically hypnotizing, but the over-simplified view of the world they represented was almost naïve in its optimism. Once it was applied to the non-critical realities of commercial development, Wright's vision seemed to have degenerated into suburbia, while Le Corbusier's vision of a 'radiant city' degenerated logically into impersonal landscapes of

Figure 5.2
*Zoning and Modern Form, accord-
ing to one of Modernism's most
virulent critics, Leon Krier
(Source: L. Krier, in New
Classicism[12]).*

repetitive tower blocks that gave no sense of orientation for
their inhabitants.

Eventually, the Modernist project started to show its misconceptions. The philosophical and existential schism between man
and his environment that resulted from Descartes and Newton's
ideas had taken a physical form: segregated cities, vague open
spaces, impersonal, rigid and over-rational housing projects
attempted to bring order into the life of the masses, with general
failure to touch their souls (Figure 5.2). In 1961 Jane Jacobs
published her eye-opening *The Death and Life of Great American
Cities*,[5] which soon became, with Robert Venturi's 1966
Complexity and Contradiction in Architecture,[6] a highly influential
marker text towards the destitution of the Modern vision. The
mal du siècle, the alienation described by Marxist critique, came
to a symbolic expression in the demolition of the award winning
Pruitt–Igoe housing scheme in St Louis in 1972, after a decade
of unfruitful salvation attempts. This date marks, for most historians, a conventional starting period of what some call the
'postmodern' or the 'post-industrial' age.[7]

Postmodernism or relativity misinterpreted

The next two decades were marked by reactionary movements to the modernist and constructivist projects, from literature and philosophy (represented by Derrida, Baudrillard, Calvino ...) to architecture. Here again, the reaction produced many antipodal schools, broadly categorized as 'postmodern deconstructionists' (Tschumi, Eisenmann, Libeskind, Hadid, Coop Himmelbau ...) and 'neo-traditionalists' (A. M. Stern, Porphyrios, Rossi, the Krier brothers, Graves...).*

*This categorization is a simplification. Different architects at different moments adopted varied degrees of classicist or deconstructive discourses. Two good sources on the subject are Papadakis *et al.*,[8] and Papadakis and Watson.[9]

> There is an aimlessness in architecture today. It is expressed by oppositions like Modernist vs Post-Modernist, functionalism vs historicism, rationalism vs eclecticism, and so forth. Behind an endless variety of similar contrasts, however, there lies an underlying anxiety: are architecture and the city disciplines, or the battleground for competition and conflicting opinions?[10]

While it is easy to find relativistic influences in the postmodernist discourse, where value and meaning lose all

Figure 5.3
Pastiche in Beirut, 2001.

absolutism, neo-traditionalists seem to cling to a Newtonian rationale where formal determinism is presented as the sole creator of a 'valid' urban setting.

The nihilism of the former and the academicism of the latter have produced equally critical environments: *laissez-faire* relativism and frivolous eclecticism produced 'instant environments' that lost all value to the whims of fashion (Figure 5.3). Neo-traditionalism and Critical Regionalism are becoming further dogmas that threaten heterogeneity and, in certain extremes, social cohesion itself:

> The emergence of a European economic union is coupled, in paradox, by aggressive assertions of nationalism. Consider for example, what is already happening in those nations lately released from the grip of Russia – Hungary, Poland, Romania – where architecture is seen as the most potent means of restoring and representing the national identity. Students are encouraged to resurrect ancient mysteries, that is to imagine objects that may unwittingly reinforce racial and tribal differences. In spite of good intentions, the monsters may return. Critical Regionalism seemed at first a benign proposition but is now proving to have a sinister subtext. ... Architecture must hold its place in this maelstrom of mediated reality that will increasingly try to dislocate the future. It cannot all be left to television ... to construct the present only from the past is to condone the death of the future.[11]

The split is evident in both approaches' relation to the new technologies of the electronic age. One of them totally ignores its implication in our lives and those of the coming generations, producing designs that are invariably 'stuck in time', in the present, looking at the past, while the other blindly jumps into conjectural design almost losing touch with practical reality.

In such a context, architecture and urban design students are forced to choose between two visions: a postcard city frozen somewhere two centuries ago, and a 'SimCity'* made up of fleeting virtual images *possibly* inhabitable two centuries from now.

*SimCity is a popular computer simulation game whose aim is the building and management of a city.

Once out of school and into the world of professional practice – out of the frying pan and into the fire – these visions become a landscape of bland imitation of sub-traditional form in repetitive commercial projects, and a showcase of architectural objects with no urban cohesion in the global arena of corporate image.

The opposition between the different schools of thought, interestingly parallel to philosophy's historical clash between intellect and intuition, reason and feeling, machine and nature, has wasted too much time and too much energy. In this context of clashing *'isms'*, a synthesis needed to be found.

interlude:

cities
and worldviews
and cinema

Cinema, from its earliest days, has been a wonderful medium for projecting worldviews in the form of screen cities. In particular, many science-fiction films have given exacerbated form to the city within the different paradigms they portrayed, while simple fiction or historical movies have just romanticized it.

Fritz Lang's *Metropolis* (1927) comes to mind first. This early German expressionist movie remains one of the most violently visual representations of the mechanical/industrial city, with its towering ghost-like skyscrapers linked by bridges, biplanes and zeppelins, looming over an underground world of machine-like workers. A few decades later, the modernist take on the city was represented by the risible (yet highly enjoyable, at least aesthetically) screen adaptation of Ayn Rand's *The Fountainhead* (King Vidor, 1949), also in glorious black and white. In the age of technicolor, Hollywood moved to historical dramas, recreating the most grandiose of settings to represent the Roman urban lifestyle centred (apparently) on the arena (there wasn't enough spectacle in the forum). Stanley Kubrick's *Spartacus* (1960) is a great example, and of course its 1990s descendant, *Gladiator*, which was directed by Ridley Scott (2000).

Scott also gave us the epitomous screen version of the extreme pessimistic postmodern city. The Los Angeles of *Blade Runner* (1982), with all its messy chaos, is a futuristic Chinatown – actually it *is* China, but with giant Japanese electronic advertising billboards and pyramid-like mega-towers. Its dust-corroded downtown buildings are constantly shrouded in darkness, and when they are not manufacturing or hunting humanoid 'replicants', its people scream at each other in a mishmash of Western and oriental languages. But that was the early 1980s; a 'lighter' take on the postmodern Heteropolis comes from the mid-1990s. *The Fifth Element* (Luc Besson, 1997) borrows the sky-avenues from *Metropolis*, but replaces the biplanes with wheel-less yellow cabs, and the zeppelins with a jet-engine propelled flying Chinese boat (for home delivery of Chinese food of course). It's all very

French and cartoon-like. Which is also the case in Jacques Tati's *Mon Oncle* (1958), which confronts the 'house as a machine' to the livelihood of rural towns, with a lot of behavioural connotations and support from the soundtrack ...

Batman (1989) and *Beetlejuice* (1988), both directed by Tim Burton, are based on comic-book originals. The former is set in another sinisterly dark city, the aptly named Gotham City, with its take on a gothic worldview of Good and Evil brought into the twentieth century. The latter opens up with a (almost) caricatural version of suburbia, with perfect little houses in perfect little gardens, and a toy-like set of colourful cars lining up every morning at the exact same time on the way to the city and back in the afternoon. A less dramatized version of perfect little lives – although no less dramatic – can be followed 'live' on *The Truman Show* (Peter Weir, 1998), set in the most perfect little town of Windsor. In the film, the little town in question is 'the world's largest stage set', englobed in a giant dome beyond which is reality. Truman does not know that, because his world is complete, with a fake ocean, fake moon and fake weather. It is only when a stage light falls on his head in the middle of the street that he realizes something is wrong. I doubt anything will fall on anyone's head in the 'real' Windsor, which is a New Town in Florida designed in 1989 by the champions of New Urbanism, Andres Duany and Elizabeth Plater-Zyberk.[1]

While the Americans were making film-like towns and cartoon-like films, the Japanese were making film-like cartoons. *Manga* films are extremely detailed, action-packed, well-scripted, feature-length animations. The unmissable *Ghost in the Shell* (Mamoru Oshii, 1995) has the most atmospheric rendering (not to mention the soundtrack) of the megalopolis of the Far East, Hong Kong and Tokyo. Another brilliant *Manga* film is the less known *Wings of Honneamise* (Hiroyuki Yamaga, 1987). This sumptuous movie has the particularity of describing a world where the scientific revolution has not brought about any form of mechanization. It is set in a culture where

space travel has become a possibility, but where
even the manufacture of spaceships remains an
artisanal craft. This means the whole aesthetics of
the city of Honneamise are extremely craft-like:
cars, buildings and everything else (down to the
electric lampposts) are beautifully detailed without
being ornamental. Without mechanization, everything
seems to have retained the memory of a human touch.

Memory itself is the key actor in *Dark City*, which
visually and atmospherically has many elements from
Metropolis, *Blade Runner* and *Batman*, while the
observer-observed concept is similar to *The Truman
Show*. In this hypnotic *film noir*, aliens live underground researching human consciousness. Through
advanced mind-over-matter capabilities, they stop
time every night and 'inject' new 'manufactured'
memories into the minds of all the inhabitants of
the city. The new memories mean, for the oblivious citizens, new lives past, present and future,
and this of course requires new settings (although
in this city the future only goes on until the
next night). This is the most spectacular part of
the film, as our aliens re-shape the city, transforming it every single night, growing buildings,
creating streets, tearing down bridges and relocat-
ing people, all in a matter of minutes. With their
control over time, space and society complete, they
then resurrect the city and lie watching until the
next project, a little like contemporary urban
designers ... who can do worse than watch the film
Mindwalk, centred on a discussion between a poet,
a politician and a quantum physicist. In fact, I
strongly suggest all readers try to find that film
on video and watch it at this point of this book.
In spite of its dated 'New-Agisms' (and an unfor-
tunate ending), it does present a good recap of
the post-Cartesian paradigm as popularized in the
late 1980s. I am not sure what director Bernt
Capra's relation to Fritjof Capra, the author of
The Tao of Physics and *The Turning Point*, is, but
you might find Liv Ullman more eloquent in her
exposition of quantum physics 101 than I am!

6
urban design
and the quantum worldview

Quantum physics is, after all a discovery or a language
used by the human mind to describe physical reality.
There is no good reason why that same language can't
be used to describe human reality if the potential for
doing so is there, and I believe it is – both metaphorically
and (...) in fact.[1]

The preceding chapters have described the close links between science, worldviews and urban form, and a similar relationship between quantum theory and a worldview based on it. With this new framework, I suggest we now look at the way we can design and live in quantum cities. We shall compose a fresh attitude to urban design within the new paradigm. This will in turn be the basis for the formulation of a methodology that would lead to a better understanding of quantum urbanism.

You might not agree with the interpretations proposed here, and you are welcome to build your own based on the unusual reality quantum theory seems to expose – whichever the case, I am certain that you will find yourself unable to see the world in the mechanical way any more as you start to recognize, in the new language, concepts you always felt intuitively. Eventually I hope this will inspire you to develop, or at least help you find the words to express, your own 'quantum' theories of the city in the twenty-first century.

First Generation

We are of the first generation in human history where the wisdom of our fathers will be of less practical value to our livelihoods than the knowledge produced during our lifetimes.[2]

Communication is at the base of what is probably the most irreversible process accessible to the human mind, the progressive increase of knowledge.[3]

Almost by definition, the quantity of knowledge in the world has been an incremental matter for millennia. Except in major cataclysms, natural or man-made (such as dictatorial suppression), humanity has added to its knowledge with time, through continuous discoveries and inventions.

The Scientific Revolution has merely accelerated the rate of growth of new knowledge exponentially over the last couple of centuries, but that in itself is not a major novelty. Early forms of information storage media, from ancient wall paintings to illuminated manuscripts, slowly became mass distribution media, from Guttenberg's printing press to satellite TV and the Internet. The major change is the accessibility factor, which has grown even faster than knowledge itself. The novelty is therefore the sudden accessibility to information and knowledge that has come to define our generation.

To Descartes' 'I think therefore I am', a CNN slogan ripostes 'You are what you know'. In other words, there is no need to *think* any more, you just *are*, because, well – *you know*. And the quantity of information that is now accessible to our generation, at least in the digitally connected parts of the world, if we are to believe CNN's slogan makes us *be* much more than our parents.

Let us not go into an Orwellian critique of the situation; rather, let us try to understand the meaning of this. Ours is a truly unprecedented moment in the history of the known universe. Not only is the wisdom of our fathers less and less crucial to our practical life, our generation's own 'wisdom' is also more and more important to *their* well-being. We are of the first generation to be able to teach our parents more than they were able to teach us, at least quantitatively. We know more because we have access to more information, even if the quality of information is not always of the highest calibre. We also know more because we have had to learn to use unprecedented technology for the collection, storage, distribution and retrieval of information. From the programmable video recorder to desktop PCs, handheld mobile PDAs and VR goggles, we have grown at home in a technophobe's hell. And we have learned to rely on it for our everyday existence; we are willing to accept the sudden crash of our operating systems, as long as we can reset them quickly – because life without instant access to our email is simply 'not practical' anymore. To many it has even become a psychotic necessity. We have learned intuitively to recognize how to use the different interfaces between the information and us, whether a simple TV remote control or a web site navigation system. The 'practical value' of our knowledge resides precisely in this infinitely quicker adaptation to the new technologies than our forefathers, as we have had to cope with such a tremendous amount of novel 'inventions'. Think about it ... it has been less than 15 years since the widespread introduction of PCs, and yet they have become as indispensable to our practical livelihood as pen and paper. There is more computing power in a handheld PC in 2002 than there was in the whole world in 1965, and that doesn't even astonish us anymore!

We are of the First Generation then, and more generations of humans practically independent from their past are bound to follow. Our generation is unique in being at the threshold between these two worlds: that of the parents coaching their children and that of the children coaching their parents. It makes our responsibility even greater in being able to span the gap between those two worlds, the world of hindsight and that of foresight. In particular, as educators and decision makers in charge of seeding the future world, we have to realize that it is as important to preserve the future as it is to preserve the past, and that can only happen by allowing each coming generation fully to actualize its own present without unnecessary burdens. Yet it is imperative that the actualization of *each* present happens with the same rules in mind. We can never accurately predict the problems or the behavioural and thought patterns that will move the coming generations, but we can be certain that if the rate of change in technology, lifestyle and access to information continues to grow, then the tastes and expectations of our grandchildren will be almost nothing like ours. This unpredictability is at the heart of the quantum metaphor and, when combined with the urban realm as a stage for current and future existence, it urges us to re-define our conceptual attitudes.

Pictures

It is commonly said that a picture is worth a thousand words; the problem of course is to find the right picture. For a picture really to be worth a thousand words, it has to be clear enough to convey the idea but remain unspecific just enough so that viewers can use their own thought processes and their own logic to understand what it is trying to say. Many feel that a thought or an idea is much richer before it is formulated in words – as if words can never give it justice. Our mind is capable of holding millions of nuances in a 'quantum superposition' of states; until we are asked to share a thought, we rarely need to use precise words to know what we are thinking about. How many times have you tried to explain *how* an idea came to your mind, especially a creative idea (suppose you were an architect who has just found the solution to your design problem) only to feel that words were failing you?

In a sense, a picture should be like a thought: focused yet open to interpretation. For ages, building cities was a matter of conjuring up a picture based on a mindset based on a worldview. And when the picture turned out to be too fixed, too literal, we panicked and thought of going back to the thousand words. We reinvented urban planning, and geography, and urban design, and so on, and tried to give each a couple of thousand words worth of definitions. In the Babel of our disciplines it has been impossible to use a common language with which to write those words, and our tower has been incapable of staying erect. Some thought they had found the solution by misinterpreting the worldview of relativity theory as one of 'everything goes', but in doing so spawned a counterculture of 'only the past goes', which has in turn spawned another reactionary position of futurism, where 'the past goes nowhere'.

I propose to go back to the 'picture is worth a thousand words' attitude by searching for a background metaphor to use as a unifying language for conceptualizing the city. Instead of forcing irreconcilable definitions down designers' throats, and incompatible designs down users' throats, we might be able to propose a new *attitude* rather than a new discipline or a new single-minded manifesto.

In keeping with the tradition of using our worldview – i.e. what we currently know or believe the world to be like – as a picture to base our vision on, we shall attempt to build the background metaphor using the conceptual language developed by quantum theory. If the images thus conjured are worth different sets of 'thousand words' to the different readers, as I hope they are, then we will have succeeded in finding the common ground on which to stand to develop further theories of the city in the twenty-first century.

Redefinitions

Redefined, urbanism will not only, or mostly, be a profession, but a way of thinking ...[4]

To be able to use the new metaphor, and because we are still functioning within an existing practical, educational and professional framework, we will need to discuss a repositioning of some of the disciplines in charge of the urban realm. In particular, I will propose a redefinition of the *role* of urban design, not of Urban Design itself. At this point a fixed definition of Urban Design itself seems an epistemological impossibility that would only fall back into the current quicksand of definitions and counter-definitions. Redefining the role and not the discipline is similar to using another one of our 'open-ended pictures' to signify Urban Design itself. Urban Design can thus retain its flexible definition, necessary for its fulfilling of the multidimensional role proposed. A similar concern will lead us to discuss a redefinition of the *urban designer* rather than, again, Urban Design itself.

The role of urban design

> There is no single definition of urban design. It is not for Government to dictate what is good urban design.[5]

Urban design as an activity seemingly has a very loose definition, and means different things to different people. While some consider it as a discipline in its own right, others consider it merely an 'interface' between other disciplines. Is it a multidisciplinary activity, or an interdisciplinary activity?

Traditionally, the most popular definition is that urban design is the interface between urban planning and architecture. In this sense it plays a mediative role between two major disciplines involved in the urban realm, but at different levels and scales. Moreover, the latter directly tackles the physical built form in unitary particles, while planning manages more 'abstract' notions such as zoning, functions, transport networks and economy. Hence urban design focuses on the urban space created through the effects of planning and realized through the physicality of architectural buildings.

If the subject of architecture (buildings, etc.) is particle-like and that of planning (policy, etc.) is wave-like, then urban design thus defined

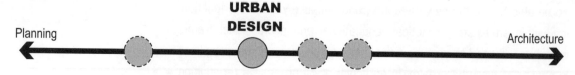

URBAN DESIGN

Architecture

Figure 6.1
Urban design as the interface between planning and architecture.

already shows notions of particle~wave duality, but that is a limited and limiting definition of its true role – although we are already beyond the pejorative definition of urban design as 'big architecture' (Figure 6.1). Yet this is the role perceived by most actors and players in the development process,[6] and it is not surprising to see it relegated to a secondary level in many real-life situations.

This misconception of the importance of urban design is due to a lack of awareness at the public, the professional and even the educational levels, of the responsibility it can and should handle.

In order for urban design to fulfil the role of a real interdisciplinary interface, it should be thought of – and taught – as a multidimensional activity. Other than planning and architecture, it should be clear that other seemingly independent disciplines play equally crucial roles in the study and/or creation of cities. Landscape architecture, communication and transport engineering, but also the 'soft' disciplines – sociology, economy, group and individual psychology and behavioural studies, even art and the humanities – are some of the poles that together shape the urban environment and give it its inherent subjective qualities.

Urban design can and should form the interface between all the relevant specialties that deal with the human and the human environment, both objective and subjective (Figure 6.2). Urban design should thus function as a multidimensional interdisciplinary interface, with the *responsibility* to manage and transform the interactions of the different aspects of urban life *into a physical and/or usable form* (Figure 6.3).

In our current educational and professional models, these different disciplines are clearly defined and entrenched in their respective

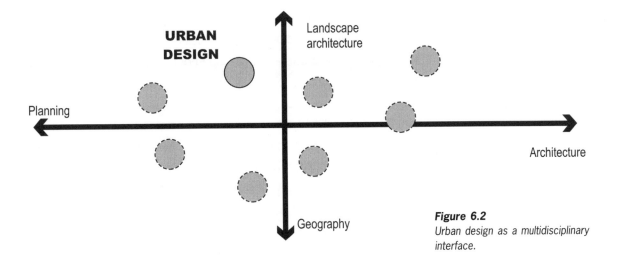

Figure 6.2
Urban design as a multidisciplinary interface.

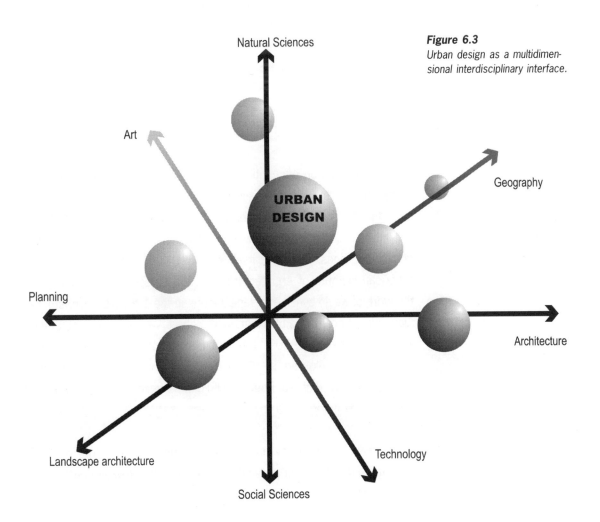

Figure 6.3
Urban design as a multidimen-sional interdisciplinary interface.

responsibilities. This is partly due to the segregationist logic brought about by Newtonian atomism and Cartesian dualism, the two pillars of the mechanical worldview that preceded our paradigm. It is interesting that this new attitude of urban design sounds so relevant to the *mended* worldview described by quantum theory. We suggest therefore an additional role for urban design: to provide society with settings relevant to its current paradigm, and to be positively active in its dissemination and adoption.

This role is not new; it has simply been an automatic, *de-facto* effect of the design of cities to be resonant with the worldview of their inhabitants. Like a work of art, the city has been designed and built with a vision in mind, and that vision has generally coincided with its contemporary worldview. With the atomization and mechanization of the professional disciplines urban design, like architecture, shifted away from art and has become a more rational, analytical discipline. Urbanists adopted dogmatic manifestos, and a self-conscious, self-righteous attitude developed within the discipline. Within the politicized discourse of the profession, antagonistic ideologies were often pitted against each other, yielding polemics instead of cooperation (see Carmona[7]).

Urban design as an occupation is relatively new, but historically it has always played the major role in forming cities. Under different guises and definitions in different periods and places, the longest lasting imprint on cities and people was due to whoever controlled the urban design decisions. The term itself was first used only in 1957, by the American Institute of Architecture. It gradually spread, mainly through the work of Kevin Lynch and Jane Jacobs in the 1960s and Christopher Alexander, Leon and Rob Krier, and Robert Venturi, amongst others, in the 1970s and 1980s. The last decade of the last century saw urban design coloured by the views and counter-views of Charles Jencks and Sir Richard Rogers, HRH the Prince of Wales and Rem Koolhaas, to name but a few ...

In all cases, many today have accepted the fleeting nature of urban design definitions as an unavoidable fact, as Alan Rowley concludes in a highly revealing article:

Many urban designers reflect a deep seated anxiety when challenged to define urban design. They long for a short, clear definition but in reality this simply is not possible. No one or two sentence definition is really adequate, nor is it likely to prove of lasting value. So it is pointless to search for a single, succinct, unified and lasting definition of the nature and concerns of urban design. It is much better to follow a number of signposts about, for example, the substance, motives, methods and roles of urban design.[8]

A precise definition of urban design is necessary only for administrative purposes, to relegate responsibilities and liabilities, and to keep legislators busy. For a designer, it is not necessary. In fact, for a 'real' designer – you know, the passionate artist in all of us – boundaries are anathema, and definitions are just that. Thoughts and pictures are not. That is why I believe a new mindset is what is needed, and that is what I hope to define in this book.

The underlying search is for the starting point of a theory that relates 'good urban design' to the *faithfulness to an organic worldview* – not to the retrograde vision of traditionalists and neo-traditionalists, nor to the nihilistic futurism of postmodernists, and not even to the numb practicalism of post-postmodernists. We will go after a synthesis of all these approaches and more, going deeper – almost literally – into the heart of the matter. We will be looking for the role of a unified worldview in the making of urban environments, beyond the formalism adopted by typical research. An urban design process that responds to the current paradigm should provide positive urban space, as long as this worldview is holistic and organic, as it was in pre-Cartesian societies, and as long as it is technological and pluralistic, as it needs to be in the twenty-first century. Because the new sciences provide such a worldview, they should be ingrained as early as possible in the minds of the different players of the urban realm.

The urban designer versus Urban Design: a new attitude

'Urban design' is a relatively recent occupation, and therefore so is the profession or expertise 'urban designer'. It is remarkable that the introduction of this new expert class at a time when Urban Design itself has such a loose definition has only added to the confusion facing young graduates at the moment of choosing their professional path. I still have in mind the welcoming speeches of the respective chairpersons when I started studying architecture in Beirut and then urban design in Oxford. The first phrase of each speech is the only thing I remember clearly, probably because in both cases it sent my mind scrambling for implications. The architecture chairman gathered the 50 or so new recruits, and proclaimed: 'Welcome to the elite'. Several years of boot camp later, armed with a state-of-the-art architecture degree, I went on to the professional battlefield only to realize the absurdity of that phrase. Looking for a new mantra, and for an upgrade of my weapons arsenal another few years later, I was aghast at the urban design Chair's welcoming speech: 'Forget all you have learnt before'. He might as well have said 'Abandon hope all ye who enter here'!

Our educational system is as atomistic as Newtonian physics ... the illogical need to proclaim the supremacy of each discipline only to break with it at the next step creates a sense of unfinished business and wasted time. The five or six years spent in architecture schools have got to be worth something to remember in urban design! And what of the years spent studying and practising landscaping, social sciences, history, geography or planning? Postgraduate urban design courses cater to professionals from all these and more disciplines, not to forget the personal and cultural experiences of each individual, particularly in international courses. Is forgetting everything and replacing it by monothematic, brainwashed 'urban designers' the right attitude? We shall return to defining a better mode of interaction between multicultural design teams in the coming pages, but let us ponder first just *who* the urban designer is.

We propose to examine the proposition 'the urban designer is the designer of the urban realm'. Let us quickly define 'design' as the act of 'initiating change in manmade things',[9] and extend it to 'change in any environment', whether physical, mental or virtual. 'Urban' throughout this book is considered to signify any human settlement, in its most generic sense. We have a tendency to equate 'Urban Design' with 'the design of the urban realm'. But while 'Urban Design' is only the professional discipline with the role defined above, the urban realm itself is the collection of spaces and buildings, landscapes and ecosystems, mindscapes and people that make up and shape any environment.

The traditionally defined 'urban designer' has a generally limited role in time, space and society. He or she typically intervenes in a finite context – for example, to propose an analysis and then a solution/strategy for the built environment. The urban designer's work is little more than an informed bet on the possible outcomes of the future development of a site. It can be a catalyst for change (hopefully positive), but in the end the real actuators of urban design are the end users themselves.

It thus becomes obvious that the straightforward proposition 'the urban designer is the designer of the urban realm' does not relate to the 'urban designer' as the class of specialists that practise the profession 'Urban Design'. Rather the urban designers of our proposition are the literal *generators* of the environment – in other words the users themselves with their continuous shaping and re-shaping of the urban realm: *the urban designer is the urban realm user.*

The professional unit responsible for urban design is the 'urban design team'. Expert members of the urban design team can themselves happen to be users of the same site under study in some cases; conversely, lay users could collaborate in the team. What should be kept in mind is that the product of the urban design team is limited and relative in time, and it is only fulfilled by the continuous use of it.

The claim that users are the urban designers is not made in the same manner as proponents of 'participatory urban design' make it. It is made in the sense that the urban realm is a constantly redesigned continuum completely interlinked with its users. In other words, the urban realm is not merely the 'container' of urban life, it is both the container and life itself, and urban design is the design of the continuum, not merely of the container. In the first democracies of Greece, *polis* signified both the city and its inhabitants; in the Arabic language,

*'Neighbour' translates as *jar* in Arabic, while 'neighbourhood' sounds like 'the container of neighbours'; in spite of its clear social connotations it remains much more spatial, as it is easy to imagine a neighbourhood without thinking of the actual neighbours. In its literal Arabic translation *jiwar* it is the physical vicinity and is not equivalent to *hayy*. Similarly, the French *quartier* (quarter) and *secteur* are decidedly spatial, even geometrical words.

the word for 'neighbourhood' or *quartier*, both with purely spatial connotations* is *hayy*, which is the exact same word for 'alive', while its plural *ahya'a* is the same word for 'the living'. This intricate relationship between the container and the contained is felt very strongly in the liveliness of Middle Eastern cities. It is even more remarkable when you realize that the Arabic language has an extremely rich and nuanced vocabulary, making the choice of words more philosophical than merely practical, especially in such cultures where Urban Design is not a common professional discipline.

The point is that the separation between the designer and the designed, the container and the contained, common to Western culture and language in the Cartesian paradigm, is similar to the absolute separation between observer and observed in classical Newtonian science, but is superfluous in the language of the quantum worldview. Yet the best-willed attempts to counteract traditional approaches of 'top-down' design have translated into little more than 'participatory urban design', branded as the secret elixir for all urban and social ailments. My own sentiment, especially from living and practising in a part of the world where 'container' means 'contained' and *vice versa*, is that in many cases participatory urban design is an artificial solution to an artificial problem. It is more often than not a localized, apologetic attempt at 'bringing the locals in', which remains in most cases based on severely patronizing attitudes and, when exported to non-Western settings, on almost colonial attitudes dressed up in orientalist clothes. The 'locals' are in whether we like it or not – whether our elitist education admits it or not. They are themselves the intrinsic ties to the space they will be living in. In other words, if they cannot have this link, they will simply either move on or destroy the place until it reflects if not their comfort at least their discomfort – and in both cases their state of being.

Participatory design tries to counteract typical top-down design by looking at the 'community' of users as a fixed, predictable mass of people and customs, and thus attempts to 'give the people what they want'. But 'nowhere in the society are people's futures mortgaged so far ahead as when the municipalities plan housing projects, earmark uses of land and build highways'.* With all the goodwill in the world, besides a few successful experiments, such an attitude remains oblivious to the fact that this community is an open, living organism that will develop in time new lifestyles, new tastes, new needs, new politics and new economies, and as such it is almost unavoidable that the next generation of users will feel alienated by the setting of its predecessor. The same sample group of people involved, say, in a participatory design workshop will provide totally different answers depending on how the questions are formulated, or even depending on whether it is a sunny or cloudy day. People are more moody than electrons, and in quantum theory electrons themselves seem to adapt their behaviour to the experimental setting!

Whenever the changeability of the current users is recognized it is looked at as transience, mainly when dealing with communities with particular identity of social class or ethnicity. The attitude then becomes based on postulates of high transience of the users, thus building generic or worse: 'universal' environments that are rigidly regulated against 'personalization' – in other words, against 'tampering'. The theory goes that the next 'wave' of users will find it easier to adapt to it this way.

By using the both/and logic and accepting that the real urban designers are the users themselves, a stronger attitude considers the users as both transient and fixed, with their environment completely and intricately linked to them at any particular moment in time. In other words, it allows the production of fault-tolerant design that accepts the changes and adaptations made to it by its users as the essence of what it is: *theirs*. Those changes do not need to be reversible (a costly and irrelevant quality), but simply re-appropriable by the next wave of users, whether of a different generation or simply of a different group or identity. In all cases, and in a long-term planning attitude, consecutive generations should be allowed to relegate to their successors a memory of their own knowledge and their own memory, as a basic need of humanity's supra-conscious continuity.

*from a report by the Swedish Secretariat for Future Studies, quoted in Myers and Kitsuse.[10]

Information storage

The subject of urbanism [is the] encoding of civilizations on their territory.[11]

The Ancient Egyptians built the pyramids as archives of memory and knowledge. From the angle of incidence of the galleries and the hieroglyphs carved onto their walls, to the alignment with the sun or with the stars, every design decision was dictated by the spiritual need to keep a record of their history and culture and the practical need of keeping time. It is perhaps a lucky break that our civilization is capable of storing incredible amounts of knowledge on one optical disk. A DVD is recorded in a few minutes and holds information equivalent to thousands of Great Pyramids.

If we were to build a pyramid or a cathedral to code every bit of information we have amassed in the last few hundred years, we would probably have no place to stand on Earth anymore. Or perhaps it is precisely the fact that we are able to quench our need for recording our present without undertaking mammoth constructions that has caused us to end up feeling so spiritually uncomfortable in most of our physical environments. In both cases it seems as though the need of a *sense of time* is what helps us keep track of our place in existence and our location in the history of humanity. Our environments used to be our archive of memory and our keeper of time. In the Cartesian world we have learnt to separate our memory and our time. In the Newtonian world we have replaced our time-recorders with mechanical wristwatches, and our memory with books, tapes and laser disks. No wonder we have reacted by creating ersatz replicas or cyberworlds as eager attempts at recovering what we unconsciously missed most: our place in a moving time. In the quantum world, we might be able to retrieve this place in time by putting *ourselves* back into space–time. Here is where lies the importance of contextualization in the society–space–time continuum, which we shall return to define better later.

Timekeeping

Timekeeping has always been a shaper of public architecture, even in its most practical aspects. Somehow the trend has been towards measuring shorter and shorter periods of time: the Ancient Egyptian temples measured seasonal and yearly rhythms, equinoxes and planetary alignments; Roman sundials and medieval hourglasses measured hours in a day. The clock tower first appeared as an urban design feature in the Renaissance, and with it the need to shape urban space in a way that allowed time to be read from as many points and as far a distance as possible. From street alignments to shaved façades designed to optimize lines of sight towards the clock tower, the city adapted to this new representation of time, which inadvertently cut the day up into still finer increments. It was the seed of mechanical time, which only matured with the industrial revolution and the transformation of time into an economic currency.

At the dawn of the Industrial Revolution, wristwatches were commonplace and timekeeping a more individual than public matter. By the turn of the twentieth century, architecture could go back to archiving technology and knowledge rather than keeping time itself. Modernist architecture was, at least in theory, a brilliant attempt at archiving knowledge by interpreting it through its technological manifestation. Modernist buildings such as Mies van der Rohe's relatively late Seagram tower are an implacable hymn to man's capacity to fashion new materials from nature, and to manufacture them effectively in quantity for the first time in history. It is also a witness of modern man's capacity for abstraction and rationalization in both thought and art. But it lacks the capacity to keep time for society, and therefore to keep memory. That becomes apparent when modernist beliefs attack the urban realm.

Modernist urbanism, particularly as represented by Le Corbusier's early work, thought to express the sense of time, but only in its present tense – the *now* of the instant free from all past history. However, in an outburst of optimistic positivism, modernists forgot to imagine a future where their own creations would become of the past tense. By thinking of the *present* as an absolute point in time, they froze history. Le Corbusier 'wanted modern architecture ... to expunge historical time from the city'.[12] It is precisely that purging of time that allowed the spread of modernism and the International Style that embodied it all around the world, independent of the societies it housed. By stripping urban space from its relative time dimension, its role as holder of memory (and therefore of identity) disappears, and it becomes easy to replicate in any context.

With the inevitable passing of time and the uncritical multiplication of the modernist vision, epitomized by the Plan Voisin for a New Paris and implemented around the middle of the twentieth century globally, something unexpected happened: modernist buildings took on an identity all their own. But unlike their early proponents imagined, it was not an absolute, neutral identity. Looked upon by purists and aesthetes, they became themselves works of art representing a brilliant but *past* moment in history. Looked upon by puritans and romantics, they became horrendous symbols of de-humanized environments. Whichever the case, modernist architecture has become as much part of our urban setting as has 'traditional' architecture. Lately many urbanists, such as Christian de Portzamparc,[13,14] Philippe Panerai[15,16] and Rem Koolhaas[17–19] have learnt to accept the equal validity of both moments (modern and pre-modern) as makers of urban space, and from that point take a conciliatory stance that is of high relevance to our quantum metaphor.

Modernist urbanism was, just as all urbanisms that came before it, a reflection of its creators' worldviews. These worldviews represented the moment's knowledge and technology. Modernism, as related to a mechanistic, determinist worldview, could not have produced better urban space. Because it spoke of absolute truths, absolute time and absolute space, it could not keep memory or time, or even shape space itself. It needed to break with the past, yet it forgot to link with the future. That is what makes it so easy to criticize today. But modernist urbanists themselves cannot be blamed for what they produced: they were honest to their own worldview.

We are lucky. We live and practise in a worldview that is conciliatory, ecological, and more hopeful than deterministic. By adopting it and allowing it to permeate our thought and design we can produce environments with which our conscience can be contented, and which our children's consciousness can re-adapt.

Model or metaphor?

When attempting to adopt a scientific theory to non-scientific areas of research, two approaches are possible: to use the theory as a metaphor or as a model.

> What is the difference between a model and a metaphor? A metaphor carries meaning beyond the obvious, therefore a metaphor is more than a theory. A metaphor can be a kind of guiding principle for thought. One could explain a metaphor as a kind of high-level analogy.[20]

A metaphor borrows a language and imagery to describe the subject of the research. A model suggests strong self-coherent laws that should permit more or less accurate predictions of the future states of a system. Since one of the present book's aims is to provide a starting point for further, more focused, research, it is more interested in the *hyper*-metaphor, yet borrows loosely from both approaches.

As a metaphor, quantum theory provides a language rich with simple concepts that permit easily identifiable analogies. This is the safest approach, since a metaphor does not pre-require experimental proof for its validity. On the other hand, a metaphor needs to be validated by its relevance and its usefulness – in other words its adaptation and scalability.

A model of the urban realm based on quantum theory requires, by contrast, extensive analysis and scientific testing beyond the scope of this work. Instead, quantum models of the urban realm will be hinted at through examples designed with what seems to be a similar paradigm in mind. Throughout the text, some ideas inspired by the quantum metaphor might perhaps trigger practical applications. In all cases, like Calvino's *Mr Palomar*,[21] I personally prefer the flexible 'model of models' to one model.

This book is not concerned with presenting a complete theory of urban design based on quantum theory; I leave that to others who might feel it is academically relevant. There is, though, some evidence as to the validity of such research: Danah Zohar has presented a solid quantum mechanical model of the human mind, followed by an even more thorough model for a quantum society. There is no real reason why a quantum individual operating in a quantum society would not be most at ease in a quantum city – that is, a city literally alive through its *urbs* and its *civitas*, whose layers of components behave and interact according to a set of quantum laws.

A model of a quantum city would actually have to take in the inherent qualities of spaces, such as memory or meaning and identity, as objective measurable and predictable variables resulting from a probabilistic set of self-coherent laws: models by definition remain limited variable approximations, and therefore should remain probabilistic overall, a quality that would verify one of the caveats of the quantum metaphor. Such an approach might even lead the way to formal theories.

Still, it is the main contention of this book that the answer to the problem of design of urban space in the twenty-first century will not be a *formal* or a *relativistic* theory, but a *relational* theory based on a radical paradigm shift from a mechanistic Cartesian paradigm to an organic quantum paradigm. Therefore, no *single* theory of urban design should claim to be an exact model of the urban realm. What should be introduced instead is an overall metaphor – a 'background theory' – that links urban design thought back to that of the other activities and disciplines involved in the urban field.

The quantum hyper-metaphor

> Mr Palomar's rule had gradually altered: now he needed a great variety of models, perhaps interchangeable, in a combining process, in order to find the one that would best fit a reality that, for its own part, was always made of many different realities, in time and in space.[22]

We have defined the role of urban design as 'a multidimensional interdisciplinary interface, with the *responsibility* to manage and transform the *interactions* of the different aspects of urban life into a physical form; to provide society and the individual with the settings relevant to its current worldview, and to be positively active in its dissemination and adoption'. To establish a firm grounding to this definition, what is needed is a background theory, a metaphor-led methodology, based on the quantum worldview we have been discovering.

This proposal is not entirely new. The history of urban planning policy shows cyclical recurrences of similar concerns throughout the last century; the interested reader can follow an enriching account of the development of planning policies and theories in Peter Hall's *The City of Theory*.[23]

Worldviews have always bred paradigms and models that would shape the relationship between theory and practice. One example is the systems worldview popular in the 1970s and 1980s. It saw the world as a layering of systems, and produced a methodology that consisted of a search for computational models of the urban fabric. Not surprisingly, it had its roots in linear engineering, and soon showed limitations in dealing with the complexities of real life – as with all offspring of the mechanical worldview. Positivism and Possibilism also alternated as driving forces behind urban design theories, as fashion provided its share of ephemeral variables. The novelty of this proposal lies elsewhere.

First, it encompasses the different cycles at work (including the *Zeitgeist* theory, the policy translation, and the current fashion) under a hyper-metaphor that allows for the oscillations of each cycle. As noted earlier, a metaphor is more than a theory, and the main and most extraordinary aspect of the quantum metaphor is what has been referred to as 'the both/and logic', which permits multiple models and interpretations to coexist and still produce a coherent whole, regulated by the principle of Complementarity.

Second, it calls for a *conscious* adoption of the world-view, unlike the typical approaches that take the world-view for granted: it calls for a critical evaluation of contemporary paradigms, and its implication at an early stage of education, as a common background to any particular model or theory. This proactive approach is necessary, for the rate of change and the degree of distracting stimuli that drive our civilization barely give us enough time to resonate with our world-view and make the best of it.

Finally, it re-positions urban design as an activity with a direct responsibility in 'making the world a better place' – a *social* responsibility akin to Hillier's 'Social Space' and 'Spatial Society'.[24] This is achieved not through the imposition of a new ideology, but through its implication into so many aspects of urban life and its interaction with other activities and sciences. According to Prigogine,[3] there is a positive feedback effect between the worldview and the sciences, leading to a resonance that pushes both towards more success. Thus, urban design 'resonates' with the rest of the physical, human and natural sciences, to introduce and consolidate the new ecological/organic worldview.

It is remarkable that most examples of 'good urban design' that constantly resurface in city-related literature are to be found in historically and culturally pre-Cartesian societies (Medieval and Renaissance towns, Middle and Far Eastern cities ...). What these examples have in common is an overall unity, or coherence, that comes from them responding to inherently organic worldviews, lacking in all examples of 'bad urban design'. Modernist urbanism has been criticized as one of the main culprits in the loss of urban space. It was the product of Positivism, itself the offspring of the Newtonian mechanistic worldview and Cartesian dualism. Good urban design is the product of a dialectic relationship with the universe – on an almost epistemological level – and of a spiritually rich communion with our social, physical and natural environments.

Applying the hyper-metaphor to itself, we can say that the quantum metaphor is like a wave – a potentiality wave. It permeates our thought, our conceptual language and our way of looking at the world. Different situations, different contexts or projects force the metaphor to 'collapse' into one of its potentialities; it can then become a conceptual model, of use for the mapping or the shaping of that particular context only.

The next section is *one* formulation of a methodology of research and analysis based on the quantum metaphor. It presents one potential alternative to the current non-unified methods, in education and design, theory and practice. Again, the guiding idea is that a background theory, a hyper-metaphor based on an encompassing worldview, is what is lacking in the education and practice of urban design.

English, Sa'ke'j says, is a language for the eye, while an Algonquin language is a language for the ear. When he has to speak English instead of [his native tongue], Sa'ke'j feels that he is being forced to interact with a world of objects, things, rigid boundaries and categories in place of a more familiar world of flows, processes, activities, transformations, and energies.[1]

7
a quantum look to the postgraduate **education and practice** of urbanism

The need for a conceptual revolution

Unprecedented acceleration in technological advances, population explosion, and depletion of natural resources have brought a completely new set of problems to most professional and academic fields. Education and practice since the scientific revolution had responded to new knowledge by branching out in ever-narrower expert disciplines.

In particular, urbanists and urbanologists are being faced by increasingly complicated problems taxing their expertise and pressing them toward working in more comprehensive multidisciplinary teams, ranging from architects to landscape architects, from sociologists to lay users. While this collaboration is becoming more and more urgent, it seems of prime importance to assist this cooperation by developing and adopting a 'new way of looking' at the world. At the end of the so-called postmodern era, philosophy, theory and urbanology in general seem to be at a loss for unified grounds, especially after the deconstructivist 'assaults' of nihilistic post-structuralist thinkers.

At the same time, with the advent of the new millennium, scientists and sociologists are predicting radical changes in our behavioural and thought patterns – owing, to a great extent, to advances in practical technology. The Council of Europe addressed the situation in the *European Charter for the City*, better known as the Florence Manifesto of 1992:

Research no longer intends to be a general strategy to be applied on vast subjects – the territory, the city and architectural planning; it's becoming sectorial with regard to functions, bureaucratic with regard to constraints and regulations irrespective of theories, nostalgic and mimetic with regard to historical problems, formalistic with regard to problems of architectural space.

Research has taken the form of immediate answer to emergencies, avoiding to clarify the general horizon, fearing innovations and increasingly emphasizing details, separated from general models.[2]

The Florence Charter, after noting 'the inadequacy of [current] urban design as an instrument to re-create order', calls for 'a conceptual "metamorphosis" to meet the complexity of the territory with similarly complex hypotheses, where the interface of planning with real society is as fluid as possible'. Thus it not only stands in flagrant opposition to the Athens Charter, but also clearly defines the root of the problem as a need for a new conceptual language. This book proposes to base this new conceptual language on the quantum metaphor.

Urban design in postgraduate education and practice

Architects and planners often take cities and themselves too seriously; the result too often is deadliness and boredom, no imagination, no humour, alienating places ...[3]

The Modern heroic planner, armed with the Athens Charter, has failed to produce the living and livable cities built by the Renaissance genius. Le Corbusier's antiseptic functionalism has destroyed all that was human in the organic city built by time.

The overwhelming complexity of variables involved in the design, production and maintenance of the urban realm has clearly shown the inadequacy of the positivist simplification and canned solutions applied by the planners of the Modern era.

The reaction to this in the postmodern world has been a split of urban design methodology between post-structuralists and neo-traditionalists, both seeking the solution in a formalistic dogma. Neither has proved so far to have any long-term vision.

For millennia, building urban settlements had been a pretty straightforward formula: follow your worldview. If the current worldview says the stars are the source of divine power, then align your main streets with the heavens; if the Pharaoh is god, then build him an indestructible ship into the Afterlife; and if the world is a big machine and God is dead anyway, then build your cities as machines too ...

Unfortunately, building cities as machines turned out to be not too perfect an idea, and pretty soon all kinds of reactions and reactions to reactions drove urban thinkers apart – and drove them insane! In parallel, an ever-increasing development of specialist disciplines was designed to deal with the complexity of knowledge now available. Each new discipline discovered, invented or created new problems, unheard of before, that came with the typical combination of density, diversity and identity; new methods of production and of consumption, new ideas, new technologies and new diseases. The Renaissance genius only needed to think of a few straightforward issues at a time and produce designs to please one type of audience. When the nineteenth century engineer and the Modern hero were not capable of living up to his achievements, they were replaced by the technocrats and the 'experts', generally unqualified at communication with each other's discipline, and hopelessly incapable of uniting both efficient and creative decision making because of the myriad of clients and problems now to be accounted for. At one point or the other, building teams of designers as machines with independent parts also turned out to be a less than perfect idea.

The following text focuses on two important aspects of methodology equally applicable at the academic and the professional stages of urban design: multi-personal collaboration and scenario-buffered (or open-ended) design, reinterpreted through the lens of the quantum metaphor.

Renaissance genius, Modern hero and quantum acrobats

It is unrealistic and futile to look for a twenty-first century Michelangelo or Leonardo. The sheer quantity of ever-shifting knowledge that such a character would need to learn at every new project is simply super-human. Instead, today's designer unit is the multidisciplinary team. For this reason, perhaps the most essential skill that should be taught and developed in postgraduate education is what we shall refer to as *quantum collaboration*.

Currently, many urban design courses focus on group work as a central unit. Yet they fail to adopt the optimal approach to multidisciplinary collaboration. The optimal approach is one that capitalizes on the background, specialty and expertise of each individual member of the design unit. It also capitalizes on the interaction of the individual members, both positive and negative.

Such an approach is effectively described by the quantum metaphor: using the both/and logic, the team can be described as a quantum system made of individuals/experts (particles) with ideas (waves) whose interactions create an *emergent* construct, the quantum team (particle~wave duality).

Within such a construct, the individuality of each member is preserved while the emergent skill of the team is recognized. Instead of a 'group of urban designers', it is an 'urban design team of multidisciplinary experts'.

The nuance is critical: a group of urban designers whose education started by 'unlearning what they have learned' from their previous expertise (architects, planners, geographers, sociologists ...) does not automatically produce a qualitatively better design than a single urban designer given enough working time. A quantum team of cross-disciplinary individuals comes much closer to covering the various experiences and points of view of its members.

A quantum team operating within a unified framework comes closer, as a design unit, to the one-man team, the Renaissance genius, who produced so much quality urban space. Not only that, it does so not by mimicking past approaches but rather by following ever-adaptive, dynamic and creative problem-solving techniques. Like a modular software program, its members can be 'updated' or replaced with different or new information without troubling the efficacy of the whole team. The traditional group of urban designers, in contrast, represents qualitatively nothing more than an individual monothematic expert.

Add the multiplicity of cultural backgrounds in most international urban design courses, and the global market situations in real-life practice, and the metaphor becomes even more relevant.

Moreover, the very definition of the quantum metaphor permits even the most clashing of skills or personalities (a frequent situation in both education and practice) within the team to be a source of creative energy. What must be taught is the ability to manage teams through mutual excitation and balancing. Using Nobel laureate Ilya Prigogine's metaphor, a quantum team is a self-regulating complex system thriving on the edge of chaos, 'delicately poised between chaos and order': if it is too homogeneous it will fade out and die; if it is too chaotic it will break apart.

Funambulists walking the edge of chaos, the members of a quantum team are fine acrobats. They need to juggle with immense amounts of tricky information, and produce a design that is worth their name. Just like trapezists flying in mid-air, they need to synchronize their jumps carefully – too energetic and they might knock their catcher off his or her trapeze; too slow and they might not make it to their catcher's arms. They need to function with total trust in the team, but with equally high confidence in their individual selves. And they need to think fast.

> Each member of an emergent relationship finds him or herself enriched by participation in the collective, able to draw on skills or knowledge beyond his or her individual capacities. Anyone who has ever had a creative idea will have experienced something of its having come from 'beyond' the self ... The simple fact of participating in a brainstorming session has some of this effect. Everyone in the session is 'sparked off' by the thinking of the others.[4]

That also points to the importance of charettes in the bringing forward of truly inspired proposals and solutions to urban design problems (see Kelbaugh, 1997[5]): a quantum team of specialists is brought together in situations where time pressure and competition (between team members as well as between teams) add up to bring the system 'far from equilibrium' and into creative solutions.

International think-tanks function according to a similar pattern. One professional organization, MG Taylor Corporation, claims to offer 'new ways of working in the Information Age'. Among its tools and techniques it has developed 'Fundamental Principles of Collaborative Design',[6] which insists on uncertainty principles, recontextualization, and the complementarity of individual experience and group experience ... It defines creativity as 'the process of eliminating options', and postulates that 'every individual in [the group] already possesses the

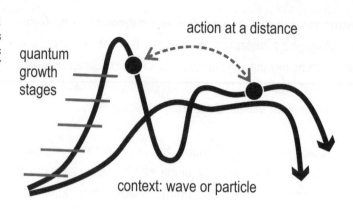

Figure 7.1
A simplified version of MG Taylor's
'Quantum Mechanics and Stages
of an Enterprise' diagram.[7]

answer'. The purpose of this intensive interaction is thus to stimulate 'one, several, or all of us to remember and extract what we already know'. Using metaphors borrowed from quantum theory, MG Taylor's principle agrees with Zohar's quantum model of the brain, where multiple ideas coexist in a quantum wave until one idea or solution collapses the wave function and realizes the thought. MG Taylor's website further proposes a 'Quantum Model for Enterprise Management'[7] (Figure 7.1) as well as a proposed approach to the 'Philosophy and Practice of Architecture'. With a language heavily coloured by fractal and chaos theory concepts, we learn that 'most organizational transformation is doomed from the outset because the culture represented by the built environment reinforces an old way of work and thought, and inhibits the expression of collaborative group genius and individual excellence as well'.[8]

MG Taylor goes on to propose a design/build/use model[9] that transcends both the traditional linear model and the current trend of feedback driven models to give a trialectic feedback overlap model. It effectively calls for a constant dialogue between all three main players involved in the process: the designer, the builder and the user.

Such a model, of course, seems difficult to apply to real-world practical solutions ... yet in our new realization that the end users are themselves designers of their own environment, the trialectic model finds a way out. But for the end users to be able positively to affect their environment, the initial stage of the professional design should take into consideration the uncertainty inherent in the different possible futures of the project. That is precisely what the process known as scenario-buffered design can address.

Probabilism and scenario-buffered design

> The more adapted an organism to present conditions, the less adaptable it can be to unknown future conditions.[10]

Most (if not all) real-life design conditions operate within a fixed economic, socio-political and morphological setting – a closed system. At least, that is how design professionals and their clients more often than not perceive their context. Traditional planning techniques are more interested in the actual, immediate state than in dynamic potentiality. The result is often projects and places that are 'dead on arrival', because by the time they are implemented, or in the best of cases by the time the next generation of users takes over, a whole new scenario will have developed. According to Stewart Brand, 'there is a tool, not used by the design professions before, that could be useful to a city planner'[10]. That tool is called 'scenario planning' (Figure 7.2).

First developed in the military in the 1960s, scenario planning evolved into strategy planning for large enterprises operating in the turbulent business environment of the 1980s and 1990s. Going beyond traditional 'programming' or 'brief preparation', scenario planning produces strategies rather than plans. 'Where a plan is based on prediction, a strategy is designed to encompass unforeseeably changing conditions. A good strategy ensures that, no matter what happens, you always have maneuvering room.'[10] Shell Oil was one of the first corporations to use scenario planning effectively, and in the 1970s, when the oil producing Arab countries decided to turn off the taps to pressure pro-Israeli countries, Shell was the only oil company that had considered a contingency plan in case of this improbable scenario and was able to make profits at a time when all its competitors registered terrible losses.[11]

This attitude corresponds well with the uncertainty principle declared by the quantum metaphor. It actually acknowledges that the analysis, design and production of urban form is not an instantaneous process – far from it – and that within the span of time needed the system (or context) goes through unpredictable change influenced by external, and equally unpredictable, forces.

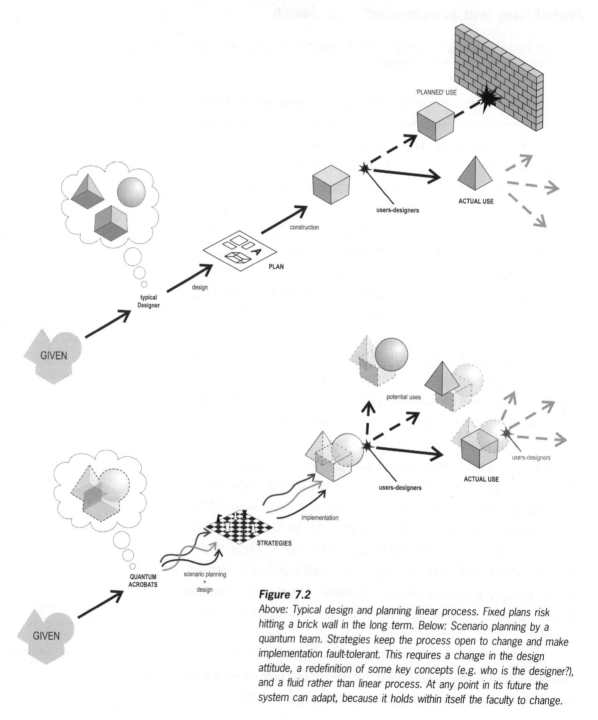

Figure 7.2
Above: Typical design and planning linear process. Fixed plans risk hitting a brick wall in the long term. Below: Scenario planning by a quantum team. Strategies keep the process open to change and make implementation fault-tolerant. This requires a change in the design attitude, a redefinition of some key concepts (e.g. who is the designer?), and a fluid rather than linear process. At any point in its future the system can adapt, because it holds within itself the faculty to change.

From this point, the main objective of the 'pre-design' stage becomes not merely the description of the current (fleeting) state of the system but rather the analysis of the driving forces (both actual and eventual) that shape it – ranging from changes in technology, regulation, competition and demographics to social and economical changes. In the language developed below, it is the analysis of the *interference* patterns, not simply of the fixed physical setting, and the estimation of the probabilities of the different possible futures; it is the development of the potentiality wave of the system.

The methodology proposed by Brand in his book *How Buildings Learn*[12] is to identify and sort these probabilities by order of uncertainty 'because it is the important uncertainties that will drive the scenarios apart'. The next step, similarly to 'catastrophe planning', is to build 'plot lines', or scenario logics, on extrapolations based on the possible interferences of the driving force. A matrix of combinations of options is drawn up, and then the design unit 'starts thinking the unthinkable'.[10]

In extensive brainstorming sessions, the urban design quantum team described above produces a series of scenarios, from the most plausible to the most farfetched. Thanks to the variety of the group's individuals, the basic scenarios cover a wide range of problems.

Brand advises the groups to stop at that point and 'sleep on it'. This is necessary for the brain literally to 'cool down' and take in the implications of the different ideas proposed during the day. It also allows the emergence of individual insights, as each team member gathers his or her thoughts without external stimuli. Zohar, who has specialized in spreading the quantum word even to management seminars, proposes in her *Rewiring the Corporate Brain*, that 'when we relax, when we sleep, ... this is when we suddenly see the whole picture, when things fall into place. ... during sleep mind reunifies itself. Awareness makes contact with the ground state, or full potentiality of consciousness.'[13]

The next day is spent revisiting (and often radically adjusting) the preliminary scenarios, of which two to five are retained. Then a strategy is developed that permits *all* the scenarios – in other words, a strategy that accommodates the common denominators of all the scenarios. An interesting approach is to proceed with a 'regret analysis' asking: 'What if we got it wrong? What would we regret not having done? What would we regret locking in?'[10] This is more than simply figuring out the worst-case scenario, or the worse possible outcome of whatever rules we have created. It is about making sure our scenarios actually cover as many potentialities as possible.

The team then repeats the process between fixing the strategy and planning out the scenarios a few times. This is because the strategy chosen itself produces new rules for the scenarios – an effect reminiscent of the 'observation method' (WYSIWYLF) dialectic described in Chapter 3. The goal is to 'get a set of scenarios and a strategy that make sense with each other'.

Finally, a measurement method, or set of indicators, should be devised to monitor which scenario (if any) is really happening. This means post-production analysis, which is currently rarely undertaken by commercial designers, for logistical purposes. Public clients, on the other hand, thanks to the very nature of their administration (city councils for instance), should find it easier to implement. This in turn implies that the communication of the strategy and the different scenarios to all involved, directly or indirectly, in the policy, design, financing, production, use and management of the project must be assured. That is because 'subsets of the overall strategy need to be devised at every level'.

The designer, builder and user remain connected throughout the lifespan of the enterprise. It also requires that the products of this collaboration be stable enough to provide day-to-day integrity, and flexible enough to allow radical, rapid redesign to fit the changing needs of the user over time. It means that the environment is never 'finished' and that it is constantly able to provide a 'just enough, just in time' solution. Things that are 'finished' in our emerging world are dead.[7]

What all this means, of course, is that the design process itself stops being a finite act in space and time, and becomes a truly adaptive process that is as responsive to past and present conditions as to possible future ones. Recently, planning disciplines have been rediscovering their need for future-oriented skills, but the product remains 'only bland and cautious truisms or blue-sky wish lists ... packaged for public consumption'.[14] The need for a clear-headed approach to foresight design is about neither short-term preservation nor futurist utopianism. In the words of Kevin Lynch:

> Our most important responsibility to the future is not to coerce it but to attend to it. [...] Collectively, such actions might be called 'future preservation'. Just as an analogous activity carried out in the present is called 'historical preservation'.[10]

Lynch's statement inspires a reflection on temporal contextualism, and provides an insight to another possible reason that makes many look at 'traditional' environments as 'better' urban design than modern ones. It seems we keep falling into a Newtonian attitude where the Past, the Present and the Future is each an absolute of its own, with fixed boundaries and event horizons: traditionalists, modernists, and futurists each fight for their part of the time-cake, forgetting the past–present–future continuity and its dynamic relativity.

In the context of the society–space–time continuum described further below, it is arguably clear that the rate of social/behavioural/economic change in pre-industrial times was much slower than the fantastic evolution that has come to affect even our thought patterns. Traditional cities were built according to visions that remained more or less relevant even during the greater time of designing and building. Hence the city's development was quite synchronized with its users' expectations, and this created an overall effect of integrity lacking in many modern – and particularly, commercial – urban products.

If Kevin Lynch's advice is of any value, we must therefore avoid simply taking fixed decisions, even decisions to choose the 'safe' approach of building in simili-traditional style. The rate of psychological change brought about mainly by unforeseen technology and communication systems means man is evolving – shifting in needs and values progressively faster than his environment. The lack of 'synch' is due to a design environment that is trying to catch up haphazardly with that extraordinary dynamic. The result is again demonstrated in the two schools of thought: the anarchic, futurist, trend-following and inadvertently shallow design, excessively chaotic and incongruous; and the traditionalist, conservative and utterly dull 'New Urbanism' that, when attempted by less than scrupulous commercial developers, risks a full scale homogenization that debilitates its future users. While the former moves too fast the latter moves too slowly, and both fail to grasp the signs of an eventual cultural/environmental clash.

The cognitive scientist Robert Ornstein and the biologist Paul Ehrlich see, in their *New World, New Mind* that 'civilization is threatened by changes that take place over years and decades, but changes over a few years or decades are too *slow* for us to perceive readily'. They insist that the solution begins with a qualitative change in the way we think and work: 'the world that made us is gone, and the world we made is a new world, one that we have developed little capacity to comprehend'.[15]

Whether the changes are too fast or too slow for our minds and our disciplines to comprehend, the problem remains one precisely of synchronization. We need to re-synchronize ourselves with our worldview. The brilliant Danish thinker Tor Nørretranders proposes that:

> ... a new form of education and training must help new generations to learn to apprehend the world in a way that is relevant to the problems the world is facing. Schools and universities will have to tell students about visual illusions, unconscious experiences, and how to 'adapt to change'...[16]

Nørretranders knows that we need 'a genuine, necessary strategy, certainly, which corresponds completely to the fact that the scientific-technological tradition is an absolute necessity if we are to solve the ... problems created by the scientific-technological tradition'. It is precisely in this outlook that the re-synchronization with our worldview can and should begin with a conscious adoption of what the scientific-technological tradition has been discovering about our world.

As each discipline consciously converges towards that unified worldview, a double re-synchronization can begin to happen. Professionals and decision makers will find a more eloquent language to communicate with, and eventually to solve a wider range of contemporary problems. In particular, urbanologists and professionals of the urban realm will be able to use the new language better to shape the city in the twenty-first century.

We will now develop a reading of the urban realm based on the quantum metaphor. It is argued that the way to 'good urban design' is the re-synchronization between users and their environment, made possible by the re-synchronization between the designer/decision maker and the worldview. The key to such an approach is through a simple yet powerful new conceptual language that uses man, nature and time as seminal construction blocks of a successful environment.

If there is to be a 'new urbanism' it will not be based on the twin fantasies of order and omnipotence; it will be the staging of uncertainty; it will no longer be concerned with the arrangement of more or less permanent objects but with the irrigation of territories with potential; it will no longer aim for a stable configuration but for the creation of enabling fields that accommodate processes that refuse to be crystallized into definitive form; it will no longer be about meticulous definition, the imposition of limits, but about expanding notions, denying boundaries, not about separating and identifying entities, but about discovering unnameable hybrids; it will no longer be obsessed with the city but with the manipulation of infrastructure for endless intensifications and diversifications, shortcuts and redistributions – the reinvention of psychological space.[1]

8
quantum analysis
of the urban realm

At its most basic definition, urban design is the design of public space. A more accurate nuance defines it as the design of *urban* space.

To begin with, a distinction should be made between 'public space' and 'urban space'. While 'public' as an adjective provides connotations of territoriality, as in the distinction between private and public functions and areas, it also contains political and economic connotations related to ownership patterns, financing, and development policies. Another layer of meaning makes 'public space' the realm of the community, as opposed to the 'private realm' of the individual. In all these senses, 'public space' speaks of the geo-politics of separation, of distinctions, limits and, to a certain extent, of exclusion.

When referred to as 'all space between build-ings',[2] it brings up images of linear stage-sets that deny urban design of its real dimensions.

'Urban space', in contrast, includes 'public space' and non-'public space' in all its meanings: it is privately owned and publicly owned space, the physical buildings themselves in space, and the space in-between them. It holds concepts of sociological and lifestyle patterns (urban, suburban, rural, sacred, secular ...) that also relate to physical and human densities.

Yet even this definition seems to limit the inter-est area of urban design to a spatial field. While any attempt to link disciplines automatically involves the spatial dimension, as Weyl argued that 'Nowhere do mathematics, natural sciences and philosophy permeate one another so intimately as in the problem of space',[3] Hillier has shown that space inherently holds a social dimension, and history has shown that time is the most necessary ingredient in the making of good urban design.

In past chapters, we have addressed the importance of time in the existence of society. Space and time have themselves, since Einstein, been known to be unified in the space–time continuum, while society and space have been in correspondence for even longer.[4] What does all that amount to in the quantum metaphor?

Open systems

The first issue we need to come to terms with is that the urban realm is an open system, and any part of it is itself an open system incapable of existing in a state of self-contained exclusion. Opening the system is the only way of allowing it to self-regulate and avoid imploding by excessive entropy. While closed systems invariably tend to a state of equilibrium represented by the most probable distribution of their constituents, which is minimum order, open systems can find a dynamic equilibrium that allows them to regulate their energy into a creative order. Any living system is an open system, and the city in particular is a living organism. While mechanical thinking can easily model closed systems, it is incapable of handling open systems. The quantum metaphor, on the other hand, involves open systems in a holistic inter-relationship.

Duality not dualism

One of the most important aspects of the quantum worldview is the concept of tolerant complementarity, or the inclusive both/and logic of duality that replaces the mutually exclusive either/or logic of Cartesian dualism.

The urban realm consists of sets of coupled categories: public and private space, public and private properties, urban and rural, community and individual, object and subject, man and context, natural and artificial landscapes, physical and cognitive spaces, form and function, sign and message, mass and void, and so on. The traditional analytical framework has looked to these couples as *dualisms*. Any part of the urban realm could be described as belonging to *either* one category *or* the other, but never to both simultaneously. Although transitional categories were introduced as they appeared in some systems (urban:suburban:rural) or (private:semi-private:public), these remain either/or sets (Figures 8.1, 8.2). This approach makes sense in a mechanical/atomist worldview, where nothing can conceptually belong to opposing notions.

Figure 8.1
A typical dualism: description is always black or white.

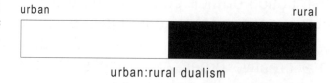

urban:rural dualism

Figure 8.2
Sometimes a transitional category is introduced, but it remains an either/or set.

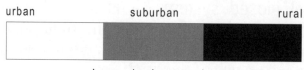

urban:suburban:rural set

A quantum reading of many of these couples shows a conceptual similarity between them and the (particle:wave) couple. If we define a particle as a localized entity limited in space and time, and a wave as a non-local notion covering unlimited areas of space and time, then it is easy to draw parallels between the (particle:wave) couple and (individual:community), (private:public), (mass:void), (form:function), (man:context), (building:city), (local:global), and so on.

If we take it further, and think of a particle as a fixed quantity and a wave as a dynamic quality, then (particle:wave) compares to (space:society), (artefact:meaning), (place:memory), (stones:culture), (*urbs:civitas*), (*res extensa:res cogita*) ...

It is clear that in a Cartesian dualist paradigm, each couple represents incompatible and mutually exclusive categories. Intuitively we recognize no clear separation between these notions, but our old scientific framework and analytical language limited us to systematic dualisms. This is not the case in the post-Cartesian paradigm.

The quantum metaphor replaces dualism with duality: the (particle:wave) couple becomes one complementary dual-aspect construct: the particle~wave duality.

With the new language, the constituents of a system stop being *either* particle *or* wave and become *both* particle *and* wave: *particle~wave dualities*. The two aspects complement each other, and any system can be described as both, whereas the degree to which it presents itself overall as either is a probabilistic statistical variable.

This is a difficult notion for our brains trained by years – *centuries!* – of dualist logic to get used to. But once this new construct is adopted, the urban realm regains its unity, and the full spectrum of intermediate states can be accessed: urban space is no more private or public, it is private~public; a user is no more an individual or a community, the user becomes the individual~community duality; a settlement is urban~rural and its patterns of order are spatial~social.

Similarly, no artefact is separated from its inherent meaning, and no meaning exists independently from its context; we are body~soul, and we belong to a place~culture; thanks to modern telecommunication technology, we are local~global and we spend our time in the real~cyber world ...

Let us take this further. Dualism provides simple, limited relationships between the coupled categories. In its simplest form, two dualisms, (A:A') and (B:B') provide only $2^2 = 4$ possible states a system can be in; since the choice is limited to A or A' and B or B', then the possible states are A & B, A & B', A' & B, or A' & B'. If we have a third dualism, say (C:C'), the total number of possible states is $2^3 = 8$; with a fourth it becomes $2^4 = 16$, and so on.* Let us use a simplified example.

*The eight possible states for a three set system would be: A & B & C, A & B' & C, A' & B & C, A' & B' & C, A & B & C', A & B' & C', A' & B & C', A' & B' & C'. Generally, the number of possible states for a system described by n dualisms is 2^n, always a finite number.

A settlement is to be described by the (urban:rural) and (private owned:public owned) dualisms. The four descriptions, or possible states we can observe (we are excessively simplifying here, considering that the description is epistemologically limited by the language used for the observation), are:

1. This settlement is urban, and its land is privately owned
2. This settlement is urban, and its land is publicly owned
3. This settlement is rural, and its land is privately owned
4. This settlement is rural, and its land is publicly owned.

More couples of course allow more combinations and thus more choices, but the number of these in a closed system is always limited. Using the complementary dualities urban~rural and private~public ownership, where each one of those dualities represents a smooth gradient, our settlement now has an infinity of possible nuanced states to be in. Automatically, of course, if we are looking for a fixed solution, finding it seems much more difficult. In reality, this does not mean the problem is more difficult than it really is; it merely means that the situation is more delicate and complex than we thought it was, or that our limited descriptive language told us. It means a conscious change of conceptual framework has permitted the designers to avoid a canned systematic, deterministic solution to a particular problem.

At this stage, the typical Cartesian reaction would be: if we cannot limit the description of a problem, how are we to solve it? It is the exact same question quantum physicists asked themselves when attempting to describe subatomic particle~waves. The answer was Schrödinger's wave equation, which gave a mathematical description of the system as a 'probability wave' corresponding to all the possible states of the system. The wave equation provides a probabilistic framework within which to work.

A settlement is not 100 per cent urban and 100 per cent rural at the same time; it is a complementary combination of both (Figure 8.3). However, since such a system needs to be dynamic (its form and qualities change in time), it is reductive to fix any of these percentages and use it as a known absolute. Just like Schrödinger's cat, the settlement subject of our study goes back to a smeared state as soon as professional urbanologists stop looking at it. If the system's state at a point in time is represented by a slider that can move from '100 per cent urban' to '100 per cent rural', the wave equation describes all the possible positions of the slider, and the different probability associated with each possible position at each point in time. It is beyond the scope of this book to provide the mathematical expression of such an approach, although one might imagine computer-assisted approximative models based on the Schrödinger formula.

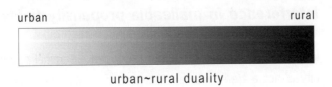

urban   rural

urban~rural duality

Figure 8.3
In duality, complementary descriptions are linked in a smooth gradient.

The Cartesian need for a limited number of possible descriptions posits a closed system, but a human settlement is a dynamic, open system. The quantum answer then is: we *must not* limit the description of an open system, but consider its 'probability wave' as an overlay of descriptions of its state, smeared in time. All this seems barely manageable for simple variable systems, and one fears that if we add the different complementary dualities at play in the urban realm, the description problem becomes infinite.

In fact, what happens is the contrary. When different dualities, each described by its quantum probability wave, are used to describe a system, their interactions become those of their probability waves. Here again, in a quantum mathematical model of the urban realm, the different formulae and variables regulate each other, and show patterns of probabilities that can predict the most probable states of an exceedingly complex system. After all, this is precisely how quantum physicists quite successfully describe quantum systems of interacting particle~wave entities.

The interference patterns resulting from the interactions of the different dualities help single out the most probable possible states in the future. This is where the open-ended, scenario-buffered design approach described in the previous chapter comes into play, as it accommodates for the most probable possible future states of the system.

In summary, even dualities themselves cannot grasp the full description of a system; it is the interference between their probability waves that tells us the most about the state of the system. This implies that in the absence of interference, it is much more difficult to map the state of a single object or event of the urban realm. This interference is the subject of the next heading.

Interference in malleable propensity fields

In 1965, Christopher Alexander produced a seminal paper entitled 'The city is not a tree', where he argues that the tree-structure pattern of thought is what produces 'artificial cities' – mostly the modern function-alist city – while the semi-lattice pattern produces 'natural cities' – 'cities which have arisen more or less spontaneously over many, many years'.[5] The logical structure of the paper was, as usual in Alexander's writing, quite convincing – to the reader of the 1960s.

In our post-Cartesian paradigm, the starting hypotheses upon which he builds his argument are somehow inaccurate. Alexander correctly notes:

> ... it is vital that we discover the property of old towns which gave them life and get it back into our own artificial cities. But we cannot do this merely by remaking English villages, Italian piazzas, and Grand Central Stations. Too many designers today seem to be yearning for the physical and plastic characteristics of the past ... instead of searching for the abstract ordering principle which the towns of the past happened to have, and which our modern conceptions of the city have not yet found.[5]

At this stage, we expect him to propose a relational principle that includes the cultural dimensions of 'natural cities'. Instead, Alexander falls into the trap of the Cartesian dualism:

> Since, as designers, we are concerned with the physical living city and its physical backbone, we most naturally restrict ourselves to considering sets which are collections of material elements such as people, blades of grass, cars, bricks, molecules, houses, gardens, water pipes, the water molecules that run in them, etc.

In the quantum paradigm, his sentence should read: 'as designers we are concerned with the living city, and *both its physical and cultural backbone*' and the list of sets should be extended to non-material elements: feelings, thoughts, ideas, memories, identity, urbanity, culture, local arts, sounds, smells, views ...

Alexander is correct about the semi-lattice structure of 'natural cities'. But professional designers will still fail to produce a 'living' artificial city as long as they restrict themselves to 'sets of material elements', because this is precisely where the authors of 'natural cities' (many of the most 'organic' of cities were somehow planned to a certain degree) differed from the modern designer: living in pre-Cartesian societies, they never restricted themselves to purely material elements as, in their worldview, *no such elements existed anyway.* In fact, once we accept the notion proposed earlier in this book that users are as much 'designers' of their environment as the professional urban design team is, and remember that it is precisely those users–designers who bring in the 'non-material elements' through their interaction with the place, the fear of never being able to design natural cities disappears.

The paper thus forms some kind of demonstration *ex absurdo* of the central theme of this book. In fact it does it twice, as he asks (my emphasis):

> ... why is it that so many designers have conceived cities as trees when the natural structure in every case is semi-lattice? Have they done so deliberately ... or have they done it because they can't help it, because they are trapped by a mental habit, perhaps even *trapped by the way the mind works* ... because the mind has an overwhelming predisposition to see trees wherever it looks and cannot escape the tree conception?

Alexander's argument chooses the second option: we design as trees because our minds work this way, and we are 'trapped by a mental habit'. If that was the case in reality, then all our design theories would epistemologically be bound to hit a brick wall.

Both suppositions are correct from within the scientific and philosophical context of the paper: the accepted model of the mind in 1965 was a mechanical/computational model, a tree-like structure. This is no longer the case: neurobiological and psychological research now adopts a holographic and a quantum model of the mind,[6, 7] while Zohar and Marshall[8] define a fundamental form of intelligence that permits re-contextualization and symbolism, and complements IQ (computational) and EQ (emotional) patterns of thought.

*Anecdotally, Christopher Alexander's latest is a four-volume work, focusing on the relationship between the organic worldview and our mental and physical patterns and artefacts (see Salingaros[9]).

In other words, our mind is *not* merely a tree-like structure, and hence *we are fully capable of designing 'natural cities'.* This optimistic thought remains burdened by our 'mental habit', which effectively has developed on tree-like thought ever since Descartes split body and soul, and Newton mechanized our world conception.*

What all this means, then, is that Alexander's argument that 'natural cities' are produced by a semi-lattice principle is essentially correct, and it is so *precisely because* it was the fruit of an age that never thought in a tree-like fashion.

The semi-lattice provides the overlap of sets and systems lacking in functionalist cities, at least in terms of physical systems. But it is only when the quantum metaphor comes into play that this structure truly gains its full potential and the semi-lattice comes alive: when the sets are no more restricted to physical elements but are extended to include particle~wave dualities, the overlaps become more than spatial systems; the overlaps of the wave aspect of the dualities produce *interference* that creates new patterns in the interstitial layers.

One way of visualizing a duality is as an *event* and an associated *event horizon* (Figure 8.4). The event can be either physical (a building, a landmark ...) or not (a happening, a fair, an accident ...), and is more or less punctual in space or time (although it can be mobile, such as a human being, a car, a periodic festival ...). However, its territory can spread to the limits of its event horizon (and sometimes further, as described under the next heading). The event is a source of waves that spread over the territory; one source can have more than one associated type of wave – for example, a building has a function, a

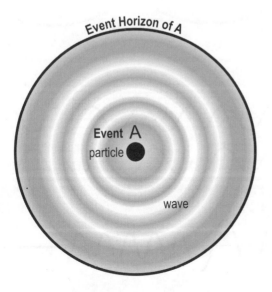

Figure 8.4
A generic duality: event and event horizon.

visual presence, casts a shadow, might propagate noise, might symbolize certain meanings, might be a magnet for certain activities, might transmit light at night, etc.

The territory is like a malleable energy field, it is filled with a probability wave that describes the propensity of the field to change (see Figure 3.5). When the event horizons of two or more dualities intersect, their waves can overlap (Figure 8.5). Interference patterns are the result of such overlapping waves. According to wave physics, three different results are possible: resonance, interference, or annihilation (Figure 8.6).

Figure 8.5

Overlapping event horizons and interference.

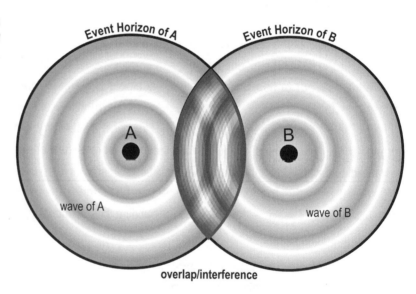

Figure 8.6

Wave interference basics. Left, resonance: wave crests and troughs coincide and reinforce each other when the waves are in phase. Middle, simple interference. Right, annihilation: wave crests and troughs cancel each other out when the waves are in opposition of phase.

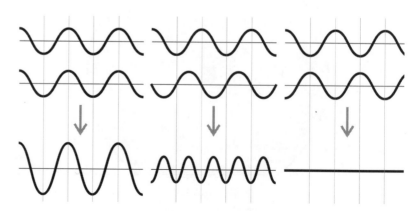

In such a model, a careful positioning of the events – the sources, or epicentres – provides the different patterns of interference. Tendencies thus either resonate, adding up to an optimal level, or annihilate each other (which could effectively produce 'neutralized' spaces, or overwhelm undesired tendencies).

The most interesting aspect of wave interference is that when two or more waves overlap, the resulting interference wave is qualitatively and quantitatively different from its parent waves. Yet, the parent waves remain intact and can reappear as soon as the overlap is discontinued (Figure 8.7). This discontinuity can be social, spatial or temporal.

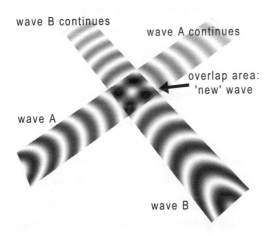

Figure 8.7
When an overlap is discontinued, if the original sources have not been altered the original 'waves' reappear.

An overlap discontinued in time is, for example, the removal of the source of one of the waves, or the annihilation of the wave by a third wave in opposition of phase. In the urban realm this could describe, for example, the effect of removing a building or a set of buildings (given that a building is a duality in that it is both the physical object and the source of a wave-like collection of properties: cultural value, function, etc.), or blocking a street visually or physically, thus discontinuing the overlap.

An overlap discontinued in space can be the simple limitation of the field or territory of any or all of the interfering waves, such that the overlap only happens in a pre-set area of space. For example, a street intersection could be seen as an area of overlap between the waves of two or more streets: past the intersection, the characteristic wave of each street emerges intact again.

An overlap socially discontinued comes from the effect of human mobility, either individually or communally, or to the scale of whole civilizations: commuters and tourists produce periodic overlaps with each other and with the other elements of the urban realm. Immigration and emigration, deportation and ethnic cleansing all create overlaps and discontinuities of socio-cultural event horizons ...

At first sight, this seems to tell us that all interference is reversible – that is, all parent waves retain constant characteristics, unaltered in space and time. But our experience of the urban realm tells us something else. Shutting off (or removing) the source of an interfering wave does not always bring back the system to its initial state. The reason for this is that waves not only interfere with each other, they also interfere with and affect the physical sources themselves. In the case of buildings, Stewart Brand[10] shows how buildings *learn*, how they change over time, altered by different internal and external events. Once the physical source is altered, the waves associated with it are automatically affected. Therefore, an interference that raises the propensity of change in some area of the field feeds back into the system. If it is powerful enough or sustained long enough it can affect

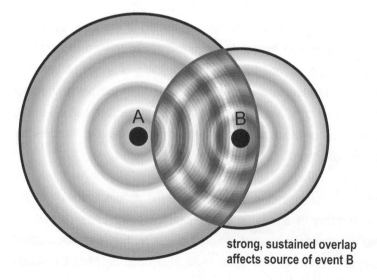

Figure 8.8
If an interference is strong enough it can affect the source itself of an event, thus changing the system irreversibly.

strong, sustained overlap affects source of event B

the source or induce the creation of new sources; hence, in certain conditions, even after the interference is discontinued, its effect continues as a new state of the system (Figure 8.8).

When the effect of an event is felt outside its event horizon, we can think of this as a non-local effect. Most of the time this effect is really relayed by the ultimate duality that is the human user and his or her memory. The user interprets and stores the information brought about by interference and acts upon it, taking its effects even beyond its spatial and temporal locale.

The human user: vessel for non-locality

The human user is a crucial duality: body~mind, individual~community, local~cosmopolitan, instant~memory and so on. Because users are also the most mobile duality and have developed long distance communication, they are here~there. They are also extremely resilient and adaptive as they interpret the interference patterns of the city.

Human users are the main actors in relaying the wave to source feedback: through their interpretation of interference patterns in their environment they act or react – from the simplest act of planting a tree (to embellish their front yard) to that of shopping (in response to a well-lit shop window display, for example). Eventually many people react similarly, building up into a resonance that can, for instance, affect the investment value of real estate, with all its physical consequences ...

In fact, every time designers (who are also human, I hope!) make a physical change they are responding (positively or negatively) to the state of the quantum field, described by the patterns of its probability wave. They thus add, move or remove events, shape or channel event horizons, and rearrange overlaps, creating totally new interference patterns.

Thanks to the mobility of individual users, local waves can create non-local interference: the users carry in their memory the information

Figure 8.9

Humans carry the effect of otherwise independent events in their memory and consciousness.

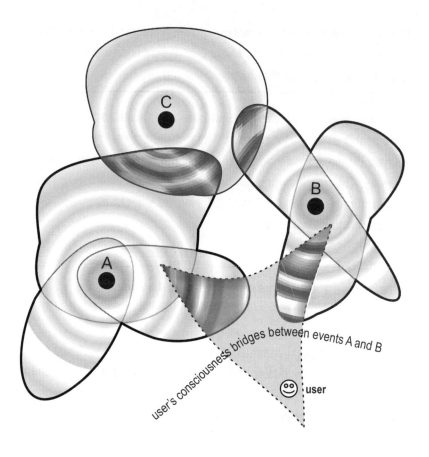

user's consciousness bridges between events A and B

user

(as idea, culture, project ...) to remote settings (Figure 8.9). This notion reminds us of the typically quantum phenomenon of action at a distance, taken to the scale of the urban realm: one potent example is the international urban design student going back home imbued with a set of values and experiences that are purely local, and adopting them globally. Another, more common, example is that of immigrants bringing their culture and way of life into a foreign land. In both cases, the resulting effect is not the pure original wave (because the original wave itself is always a composite one) but a local reinterpretation or *re-interference* of it.

The stronger the graft is, the more it interferes with its new environment. One foreign immigrant brings in enough culture to sustain his or her own memory, and more often than not ends up losing it. A large number of immigrant families resonate and recreate social and physical patterns akin to their origins. That is one way of describing cultural or ethnic neighbourhoods such as Chinatown, or gay districts ... Another more subtle non-local effect can be triggered with global communication and culture. The simplest act of reading a book or seeing a photograph or a documentary of a distant place or event (distant in space or in time or in social context) and being inspired by it to do things differently represents a non-local event (think of the propagation of the 'American dream' through television, or the periodic revivals of Greco-Roman classicism, or both – the White House replica villas in Saudi Arabia ...).

The human user introduces another major element in the interactions of the urban realm: randomness. If you toss a coin three times, even though there is a 50-50 chance of getting heads or tails it is very possible to get three 'heads' in a row. However, when you toss the coin a hundred times the number of 'heads' and the number of 'tails' is much more likely to be equal. Probability only makes sense as a statistical variable based on multiple measurements of the same event. The probability wave of each system remains only a possibility wave and not a necessity wave, as the human user individually decides to react or not to its potentiality and affect the needed change. Because of moodiness and free will, only a large number of human users inter-acting with their environment can give sense to the probabilities involved.

The society–space–time quantum continuum

The quantum individuals interfere together, and their environments. They associate into a quantum society whose cultures, memories, values, and ways of life, result from the overlap of those of its individuals. Depending on the rate and strength of individual waves, they are either diluted or resonate to create a qualitatively different society. If the new society's (or group, or community) composite wave is potent enough, it affects its physical context and/or is itself affected by it.

At every modification in any of the sources of waves, the whole system's interference patterns change. In a correct quantum model, these changes produce observable new states at discrete, discontinuous intervals: a critical mass of change energy (also visualized as propensity to change – remember the potentiality pool and its existence barrier?) – has to be reached before the system can suddenly shift states. Like the electrons of an atom jumping from one quanta of energy to the next, so does a quantum environment respond to the interference patterns of its constituent parts by shifting gears only when the interaction of its parts is at the right critical level.

In this sense, the quantum environment is more than a recipient for society, and society is more than a conceptual construct without a tangible reality. 'The city fosters art and is art; the city creates the theatre and *is* the theatre, as Lewis Mumford[11] reminds us. Hillier's worry that rational thought cannot unify society and space without some kind of epistemological concession can be settled.

> The problem is avoided, for example, if it is resolved to treat society as though it were no more than a collection of individuals, with all that is distinctly social residing in the mental states, subjective experiences and behaviour of those individuals ... Alternatively, the problem can be avoided in principle by introducing some kind of spatial metaphor at the level of society itself, usually that of some kind of quasi-biological organism in order for the metaphor to make it possible to discuss society as though it were such a system.[3]

By reuniting particle and wave, the objective and the subjective into the new construct that is duality, the 'vast epistemological chasm' Hillier describes is mended without concessions, without having to make an either/or choice. Society is both its individuals and a hypergroup of individuals that is qualitatively different from a simple addition of constituent parts. It is both what each individual makes of it in his or her psyche (sense of identity and of belonging), and the collective notion at the level of group psychology. Each individual that makes up a society has both physical and spiritual dimensions. Similarly, the urban realm is urban space's individual buildings and spaces, its individual uses and its overall use patterns, and an emergent construct that is more than an addition of the physical constituents. Both hyperconstructs society and space interact and are united at both levels of individual components and emergent qualities. This interaction, of course, happens in time. In the words of A. S. Eddington, the physicist who was one of the first authors of popular science books, 'In any attempt to bridge the domains of experience belonging to the spiritual and the physical sides of our nature, time occupies the key position'.[12]

A new conceptual construct emerges: the society–space–time continuum, stage of urban life.

The society–space–time continuum holds all the dualities and their interference patterns but, like Mumford's city, it *is* also these dualities and their interference patterns. In the quantum metaphor, no description or action of any constituent of the urban realm is possible without its co-ordinates in the society–space–time (SST) continuum. The SST continuum is an energy field of potential events. The events can be social, spatial, and/or temporal.

The term 'society' in society–space–time signifies both the physical addition of individuals and its culture, habits and symbols. The Greeks used the term *polis* to signify both the city and its inhabitants; in Arabic, *ahyaa'* signifies both the districts and those who live in them. The SST continuum concept makes it semantically impossible to separate container from contained: it permits us to think of our environments as we perceive them in reality, as our experience relates them to our mind and to our memory. Since it uses the same language our quantum mind processes use, it provides an interface to access the dual mental constructs our brain draws on to store information without having to split quantitative and qualitative data.

The creative role of the user's mind: the observer–observed dialogue

> The city is a state of mind.
> (Joseph Rykwert, quoted in Pike[13])

It is thought that our brain models the world around us by overlapping two mental constructs: perceived space and cognitive space. 'The spatial construct's strength lies in its inclusivity. It can accommodate both physical and symbolic information.'[14] Lefèvre speaks of the *espace perçu* (perceived space) and the *espace conçu* (conceived space), which are eventually expressed and experienced as the *espace vécu* (the lived-in space).* Perceived space is the mapping of external stimuli, while cognitive space is a set of internally generated information.

> Spatial constructs inform a large part of our language through metaphors and symbols. They also form the structure of our experience. Information comprising them includes visual images, sound, [heat] and touch. They all contribute to a complete and immersive sense of the world. We take information in through the senses, process it via an associative memory for interpretation, and then store it in long term memory. Expression is roughly the same, memory and thought are processed mentally and projected to the outside as voice and gesture [and action]. These expressions are in turn mediated through sound and light and enter recipients' senses as information, and once processed, enter the recipients' perceived space.[14]

This succinct description of the cognition of outer space and the re-cognition of inner space shows the importance of pluri-sensorial information to our experience of our environment. It proves once again that the urban realm is much more than physical space (mass and void, streets and squares ...). It also shows that whatever the real – physical – outer space looks like, our memory will store it through interpretation and relational thought, both affected by subjective experience.

Although we might not be aware of it, we *image-in* our context not merely through its physical, visible and tactile form, but mostly through the interference patterns of its constituents, which in turn interfere with our own thoughts, culture and past experience. When we attempt to express the image we have, we are limited by our expressive media (*How do you express the memory of the smell of jasmine in the evening?*). Thus we have to interpret once more – we interfere with our own thought – to be able to express it in a way that is understandable to our listener.

Fortunately, in our daily experience we do not need to express such complex information continuously. If we need to talk about it we can use our normal language and, in most cases, the recipient's brain will

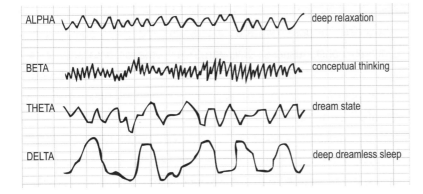

ALPHA — deep relaxation

BETA — conceptual thinking

THETA — dream state

DELTA — deep dreamless sleep

Figure 8.10
States of mind ... it's all in the waves: typical EEG brain wave patterns.

reinterpret our words into a smell or an image that relates to ours. To do this, recipients need to use their own experiences and stored relational information and symbols (*people who have never smelled jasmine will never grasp the full image, just as they wouldn't know that it was jasmine if they were to smell it for the first time ...*).

The degree to which the correspondents' images coincide is directly proportional to how much experience they have in common and their capacity at mental re-contextualization. But we have seen that each person's experience is the overlay of his or her perceived and cognitive spaces that result from the clarity and totality of information gathered from the context. Therefore it is the quantity and the quality of the *shared* information – hence, common experience – that increases social relation.

Nikos Salingaros proposes a 'new theory of urban space based on information theory and the laws of optics'. For him, the use of urban space is linked to the information field generated by surrounding surfaces, and how easily it can be perceived by pedestrians. 'So many historical urban spaces provide an emotionally nourishing environment', thanks to their optimization of visual, acoustical, and tactile signals that transmit information content.[15] His answer to 'what makes us use (or avoid) urban space?' is 'instead of some properties of empty space defined by some plan, it is actually the information field originating in the bounding surfaces, which permeates the space and connects it to the human consciousness'. Salingaros's information field acts in fact very similarly to the 'interference wave' discussed here. While he goes into the depth of the physical 'sources' of the information field, and their effect on the use of urban spaces, he stops short of linking his theory to a more comprehensive society–space–time (SST) continuum. That would have probably allowed him to see that the receivers (and shapers) of the sources of his information field – humans – themselves change in SST. In addition, their tolerance to information quantity and quality varies, allowing a dynamic 'optimization of signals' in time.

The information field he suggests connects, nonetheless, to each individual user, making him use the space more. In fact, what it also does is add to the shared experience of all the space's users, as it is easier for all of them to 'understand' it. This notion allows us to introduce the concept of identity and memory of the place into our quantum metaphor, not purely as cultural constructs, but as emergent qualities of the urban realm strongly tied to the human perceptual experience, or at least as resulting interference and resonance waves between the perceived space and the user's mind. To do this we need first to develop the idea of information fields a little more.

Information fields and knowledge media

> Our spatial environment is not only a product of thought, it augments our thought processes. We use space to make us smarter.[14]

Natural selection has shown that the most adaptive species survive best. Humans are probably the most adaptive to their environments, but even that adaptation has limitations. In all cases, the relationship between the environment and its users has long been established as a two-way interaction: our environment shapes us as much as it is shaped by us. 'Shaping' for humans is more than the physical disposition of elements and spaces. Shaping of the environment includes the addition of memory and meaning to it, and the shaping of the cognitive space inside our mind. In addition, it involves the psychological and the physical shaping of our behaviour, even if it doesn't go as far as the determinism some behavioural studies would want us to believe. Space is a field of information that our brain can transform into 'adaptation exercise'. Similar to the response of muscle tissue to physical exercise, every time our brain tries to solve a new mental or sensorial exercise, it builds up more connections and patterns and stores them in memory. This additional set of patterns can be then re-used to solve similar exercises in the future; that is how space makes us smarter.

Cognitive psychology has established a strong relationship between subjective moods and cognitive capabilities: depressed subjects have

Figure 8.11
Information overload in a Warsaw shopping mall.

more trouble learning than happy people. It has also showed that we use a buffer-type of memory, called the sensory register, to form a *veridical* image of what the sensory organs perceive. A veridical image is an 'as is' projection of the perceived space, with no meaning whatsoever attached at this stage. Although the memory of the sensory register is relatively large, it is an extremely short-term memory. Functioning as a *cache*, it must be cleared quickly to avoid superimposition of images. This happens either thanks to a rapid decay time, or through erasure or backward masking, which means new information replaces the previous one.[16] Rapid decay time leaves the sensory register (and hence the rest of the brain) in an idle state if not enough sensory stimulus is present, while backward masking overloads the sensory register in case of too much stimulus, so that previous information is erased before it has time to be processed, making cognition incomplete (Figure 8.11).

It follows that our experience of our environment and our interaction with it is strongly influenced by the quantity and clarity of the information available and by our subjective mood. If our goal is to shape our environment into something that will make us 'better', then one of the responsibilities of urban design is to allow that double shaping – both physical and mental – to happen. It is not an issue of transforming all the users into happy-go-lucky pedestrians; far from it. It is about letting them be able positively to recognize, cognize, then re-cognize the information of the environment through their different mood filters. I like to give the example of the ordered physical stimulation of Victorian streets in London versus the chaotic multi-sensory attacks of the streets of Beirut. I sometimes have the impression that the only thing that balances the sensory overkill of the latter is the extraordinary mood the blue Mediterranean sky puts one in. I think the same sun that multiplies the amount of visual detail in Beirut also allows the cognitive capacity of the user to cope with it. The same amount of information might be humanly impossible to deal with under different skies. The visual information alone seems proportional to the amount of direct sunlight available to bring out the details. This might conversely explain the much more easily graspable patterns of order one perceives in some European streets, as the design seems to adapt

Figure 8.12
Almost unbearable sensorial stimulus in the 'real' part of Beirut. What the photo misses is the disorienting aural noise.

Figure 8.13
Almost unbearable stillness in a Dutch new town. The only hint to orientation is the sound of children from a nearby playschool.

to the general weather condition, both in terms of light quality, and ... mood. In a related example, it is simple to see that the amount of simultaneous stimulus the sensory system of a twenty-first century brain can handle far exceeds that of generations that have lived without all the audio-visual stimulation of the MTV and PlayStation generation. Given enough time we do adapt to the information, our brain learns to sieve out the background noise, and raises its minimum level of tolerated stimulus (Figures 8.12, 8.13).

In this light is it really a surprise that Modernist architecture after the First World War has tried to reduce visual and physical stimulus to a minimum? Perhaps in an unconscious bid to reset its sensory registers to a normal level, after a century of industrialization, of trains, planes, automobiles, tanks and bombs, modernism went too far – resetting of the system much below the new minimum level of tolerated stimulus the war generation had by then adapted to. Could the excessive ornamentation of pre-industrial architecture be read as an attempt to create the minimum level of arousal that external stimulus wasn't reaching in those days? That other excess of the 1980s, PoMo and neo-traditional revivalism, now seems like an over-reaction to the perceived sensorial – but not necessarily intellectual – blandness of the decades before ... yet there is something that went wrong in the dosage of information and contextual meaning.

Meaning beyond function: image, identity, and memory of place

Humans seek identification. Identity rests on a duality ingrained in the society–space–time continuum: group identity and spatial identity. *Group identity* is the 'feeling that one belongs to a larger human group [based on] the feeling of shared human qualities and communality with one's fellows'. *Spatial identity* is 'based on a set of complex memories and associations of the familiar [physical] locale'.[17,18]

The link comes from the notion of 'complex memories' and 'associations': interference patterns of the constituents of the urban realm produce information. The clearer this information, the more its transformation into perceived and cognitive space is shared among its users. Hence, more shared experience, more potentially shared associations, and more common identification. Added group and spatial identification helps develop community ties, and gives meaning to the spatial dimension beyond its mere function ('home' instead of 'temporary shelter', for example).

'Meaning' is the set of symbolic values that help us construct our cognitive space. The richer the meaning of a physical space, the deeper our cognition of it and, hence, the easier its memory, and its re-cognition.

This links back to issues of cultural identity, post-war reconstruction and, more simply, to issues of 'imageability of a city', as described by Kevin Lynch:

> There seems to be a public image of any given city, which is the *overlap of many individual images*. Or perhaps there is a series of public images each held by a significant number of citizens. Such group of images are necessary if an individual is to operate successfully within his environment and to cooperate with his fellows. Each individual picture is unique, with some content that is rarely or never communicated, yet it approximates the public image, which in different environments is more or less compelling, more or less embracing.[19]

After Lynch's work, behaviourists recognized the limitations of objective observation of the urban realm. For example, to respond to the built-in limitations of research methods, which reduce their validity to purely statistical probabilities, they combine objective observation and subjective assessment: Perceived Environmental Quality Indices (PEQIs) complement quantitative, objective indexes. This need for subjective nuances to regulate any set of data is a proof of the limited accuracy of purely objective data, but does not imply that the addition of such subjective assessment will provide a comprehensive vision. After all, by definition subjective assessment is a personal matter, while indices can only be statistical. The observer making the assessment cannot claim that his or her subjectivity will necessarily reflect that of the observed; 'environmental quality' might mean something totally different to each actual user of the environment.

In all cases, when it is not the optimal amount of information/stimulus that is absent from Modern buildings, 'meaning' – or perhaps more accurately 'context-related meaning' – seems to be the main ingredient lacking in twentieth century urbanism. For example, Modernist urbanism concentrates on function rather than on the information~meaning duality, while neo-traditionalist urbanism, in its excessive faith in the atemporal value of meaning, insists on forms that might just as well mean totally different things to our children than they do to our parents today.

If meaning is what permits us to integrate our perceptions, make sense of our environment and enhance our community and our culture, then meaning is one of the main ingredients urban designers invariably need to address in their interventions. After all, if culture and community are expressions of the human mind, and are signs of intelligent adaptation, then Peter Anders' earlier argument about space making us smarter makes even more sense. Danah Zohar states an essentially similar idea through her quantum model of consciousness:

> Each of the artefacts we make in attempting to meet our bodily needs has an obvious functional purpose, and at its most primary level any object that is made can be judged a

good or bad object by whether it does or does not fulfil its function ... But because we are conscious beings with an equally strong set of needs for *integrating our experience*, for seeing ourselves reflected in our world [– *identifying* –], and for evolving towards ever greater ordered coherence in our world picture, the artefact we make must also fulfil a role of *world creation*. ... Artefacts which contain nothing of the human (nothing of human [quantum] consciousness) reflect nothing back when we deal with them. They are not in dialogue with us and they cannot meet our need for creative self-discovery.[20]

This ties back to this book's claim that what makes 'traditional' (in fact, *pre-Cartesian*) places more popular than, say, modern ones, is not their absolute form, but their 'dialogue with us', through their responsiveness to the true duality of human consciousness and in-built values: they *made sense* to their builders and users, but they also give out a sense of time, and hold within their form a memory of the worldview and knowledge of their time. That is exactly why the same building by Le Corbusier might scare the wits out of a layperson, but receive the highest esteem from the architect or intellectual who knows about the *thought* behind Le Corbusier's creations. For those who know *why* things are the way they are, and what they meant to those who made them, aesthetics and form become secondary. The required connection with our temporal selves becomes more subtle. Suddenly such environments become sympathetic to us, and us to them.

Chapter 9 will attempt to extract some implications of the quantum analysis and language to built form itself.

[All cities] exemplify similar patterns. The most basic of these is the *interpenetration of past and present*. On the one hand there is the *visible* city of streets and buildings, *frozen forms of energy* fixed at different times in the past and around which the *busy kinetic energy* of the present swirls. On the other hand are the *subconscious* currents arising in the *minds of the city's living inhabitants* from this combination of past and present.[1]
(my emphasis)

9
implications
for built form

Most aspects of the urban realm can be viewed and better described through the construct of particle~wave dualities, overlapping and interfering in a society–space–time (SST) continuum. The SST continuum is permeated by a malleable energy field, a field of possibilities that gather propensity to happen from the interference patterns created by overlapping information waves. The 'dualities in society–space–time' construct permits a mending of information and meaning, through the central role of the human user and his or her mind. The appreciation of the creative role of the human mind as the active link between past and present, between society and space, and between culture and form, leads to an ecological reinterpretation of the urban realm, and hence more humanly fulfilling environments. More comprehensive, gradient-like descriptions of these working contexts are now possible through a new semantic and conceptual extension. Combined with probability-led, non-deterministic decision making, the new conceptual framework should permit better design. A quantum model might one day propose a field theory of the urban realm, using computer-aided matrix calculations to map the propensity state of every point of the SST continuum. From such data, human designers would be able to make good predictions about the probability of events happening or not. They would then take the right measures to encourage or discourage, then to permit or prohibit, the actual future happening of a probable event.

If the new language is to be of any practical use, it has to affect not only how we think about the city, but also how we build it. The 'how' needs two answers: what *form*, and what *policy*. Policy is too variable to be addressed in this book, as it is dependent on political and national contexts, but I hope others will be inspired to propose implications of the new paradigm to policy in their respective organizational systems.

The form issue itself concerns us only insofar as it relates to generic interpretations of the metaphor, and therefore all subsequent suggestions are also purely tentative. These interpretations are mainly based on redefinitions of the 'stuff' that makes up the urban realm. They do not claim any exclusivity to the quantum metaphor, and by no means are they comprehensive. They do not say 'how' to design but rather, in keeping with a main contention of this book, point out how some design problems could be approached.

The main objective of this chapter is to show the capacity of the quantum metaphor to tackle a wide variety of issues, including possible implications of the new approach to built form, at different levels.

By definition, the background hyper-metaphor does not provide guidelines or rules of thumb: it is based on the concept of uncertainty. It suggests interpretations that could produce more integrated environments. Because of the nature of our paradigm, 'built form' will as easily signify the 'frozen' as the 'kinetic energy' that Burton Pike speaks of. It is hoped that the following paragraphs will provide a primer towards more comprehensive theories or, in the very least, inspiration for different design approaches.

In search of an axiom for the definition of 'good urban space'

> He who does not know how to vary our pleasure will never give us pleasure. [The city] should in fact be a varied picture of infinite unexpected episodes, ... a great order in the details, confusion, uproar and tumult in the whole ... Order must reign, but in a kind of confusion ... and from a multitude of regular parts the whole must give a certain idea of irregularity and chaos, which is so fitting to great cities.[2]

In the absence of an absolute definition of a 'good urban design' index (such an absolute constant is epistemologically impossible, and is anathema to our quantum metaphor, because of the perpetual need for SST contextualization), all we can offer is a suggested axiom upon which generic implications are built. This axiom results from concepts of behavioural and cognitive psychology, sociology, complexity theory, information theory, and the quantum metaphor concept of interfering waves. This sole axiom will be used to extract generic implications of the quantum metaphor to built form. No detailed 'guidelines' or recipes will therefore be produced, since that would necessitate the compilation of indexes beyond the scope of this book. Only an accurate mathematical model of a quantum city theory (including psychological research) would produce a usable set of such indexes, which nevertheless should remain sociologically and temporally contextual. With the advances of information technology and GIS systems, such a feat could quickly become a practical possibility in some localized projects.*

*For example, Hillier's process for Space Syntax analysis could provide a starting point set of contextual indexes that might be correlated to 'wave' parameters.

For those who still believe in the necessity of such scientific approximations (and those who still require scientific accuracy to judge a metaphor), it must be stressed that this by no means implies that the following text is ungrounded or useless; intuitive design within the quantum paradigm can produce good urban space based on the simple generic notes. I firmly believe that the conceptual shift from dualism to duality, and from determinism to probabilistic indeterminism and scenario-buffered design, is enough to induce a noticeable qualitative enhancement in urban design solutions without the need to develop typical 'cookbook urbanism'.

Complexity

If we carefully pour a layer of salt into a glass jar and a layer of pepper on top, when we look at the side of the jar we see two 'clean' bands. If we now close the jar and shake it violently, salt and pepper mix in a greyish volume. As much as we shake the jar, there is no chance of the particles redistributing themselves in such a way as to going back to the original, 'ordered' situation with all salt on the bottom and all pepper on top. This is the result of added entropy, or disorder, in the system.

But the jar was a closed system. We can imagine someone with incredible patience (or ingenuity) opening the jar and carefully separating the salt from the pepper particle by particle. It would take more energy than the energy it took to dissipate the order initially, but it would transform the system from a closed to an open one, and allow the resetting of the level of entropy.

While some parts of the universe may operate like machines, these are closed systems, and closed systems form only a small part of the physical universe. Most phenomena of interest to us are, in fact, open systems, exchanging energy or matter (and, one might add, information) with their environment.[3]

In the natural world, late twentieth century biologists have discovered open systems that self-regulate and give rise to higher order complexity. Dissipative systems, as described by Nobel laureate Ilya Prigogine, have a special structure that lets them borrow energy from their environment, and use it to dilute entropy.[3] Such systems are common in the universe, and are one of the particularities of living organisms. Without such a capacity for 'self-organization', life and nature in general would have been incapable of evolving into the complex forms they now exhibit.

Diversity

Only open systems are capable of developing dissipative structures; therefore only open systems are capable of complexification and differentiation, and hence of diversification. Closed systems are fated to run down and die into infinite entropy. Diversity is therefore the presence of open, living systems. Such systems thrive on the borderline between order and chaos. They are ordered complexity, and need a constant interaction with their surroundings. If closed off, they just die.

Arousal

> It seems to me the best designs are those which accommodate the most contradictions. Looked at the other way, the most boring design is that which is directed at a simple, well defined future. A lot of New Age music exemplifies this, as does, for me, Le Corbusier. They are both addressed to simple world pictures, and to simple ideas about how humans behave and what they want.
> (Brian Eno, in Brand[4])

Brian Eno is neither an architect nor a layman. He is widely considered as one of the pioneers of modern electronic music, a cosmopolitan artist who has created or produced some of the most memorable albums of the last three decades of the twentieth century. He was one of the first to successfully mix traditional musical sounds with advanced technology and instruments to create the multicultural, multi-layered sound of his generation. The work of Le Corbusier does not shock him, it *bores* him ...

Behavioural research has shown that the human brain responds differently to various degrees of arousal, which is necessary for its optimal functioning.[5] Ilya Prigogine's work[3] describes how complex self-regulating quantum systems need a 'just measure' between order and chaos to survive creatively. Bohm's insights and Zohar's research have argued an intrinsic role of human consciousness in creating the environment;[6-9] Bentley[10] has suggested *richness* as an urban design quality based on multi-sensory information, and Salingaros[11] information field theory describes human beings as 'information-processing machines whose existence depends on the ability to interpret the information present in their surroundings'; this information is optimized through a balance of quantity and clarity (or quality), or content and accessibility.

The human user is a *source* (passive and active expression), a *receptor* (passive and active senses) and a *carrier* (memory and cognitive and perceived space) of information. The user's well being and development strongly rely on the fulfilment of these three roles, through which she can develop a sense of individual, group, and place-related identity.

The present book proposes that interference patterns of potentiality waves are what the human mind recognizes – both consciously and unconsciously – as information, and the quality and quantity (density) of this information produces various degrees of arousal, defining choice, and is eventually transcribed into action or memory. By 'arousal' we signify 'stimulus', or simply the opposite of 'boredom', *in those two words' most generic sense*. Arousal affects the cognition of the environment in its social, spatial and temporal dimensions, and this cognition involves imaging and adding meaning to the image of the space. Constructive urban design creates an optimal environment for the user to wander and live in – in other words, 'good urban space' should approximate arousal levels to a contextual optimum.

We have already established the importance for humans of a sense of identity, social and spatial, individual and group related. We have discussed the necessity of diversification and differentiation for open systems and the ability of such systems to evolve into self-regulating, living organisms. We have also seen the concept of density at work in allowing interaction and interference of dualities, as well as the need for optimal density of information for the good development of perceived and cognitive space, all regulated by ever-changing human receptivity to that information. In other words, 'good urban space' should have at all times an optimal density of varied information and an optimal presence of diversity, and should allow the development of a sense of identity. We need to build from these three major concepts – identity, diversity and density – a new construct that would describe an inherent quality of such an environment.

'Diventity'

I propose to call this new construct 'diventity', and define it as such:

Diventity allows identity to continuously emerge from the density of diversity.

Identity is about self-similarity, but it is also mostly about differentiation; in other words it is about being able to recognize similarity and difference simultaneously without the risk of one aspect obliterating the other. Identity is therefore a duality by definition: it requires a sense of individuality that is constantly checked with a sense of community of others. This dual sense of self-similarity and differentiation is a characteristic of self-regulating dissipative structures, it requires an open system to emerge, and a minimum of stimulation at the initial state: open systems can develop differentiation and keep it alive through self-similarity. This is only possible through diversification and complexity. Diversity is therefore tantamount to the sense of identity, as it is through difference that self-identity is recognized.

Diversity itself cannot be described in an absolute dimension. It is in immediate relationship with the spatial and temporal dimensions: by definition, diversity only appears when different identities are brought together. This 'bringing together of diverse identities' happens in space–time; in other words, it requires a certain proximity to become meaningful. The proximity of difference can be spatial and/or temporal; two or more different identities can be confronted in space or cycled through time. The quantity of space–time allowed for that confrontation is critical; if it is too large there is no interaction between the different identities (we can now say their event horizons do not intersect), and if it is too small the difference risks being unperceivable – and this is where self-preservation reflexes appear in human identities, for instance, risking clashes or the breaking down of the system.

This relationship between the number of different identities and their space–time dimension is easily described in terms of density. The density of diversity at any point in space–time (and eventually of course in society–space–time) has the potential of creating self-regulating, differentiated patterns with a new emergent identity that is different from the sum of the component identities. When the density of diversity of a system allows the emergence of a new identity *that is different from the composite identity*, this system is said to have the quality of *diventity*.

Because the concepts of identity, density and diversity are themselves generic and scalable, diventity is a powerful new construct that is generic enough to allow comparative studies of otherwise unrelated systems (e.g. the cultural composition of the USA vs the cultural composition of Los Angeles), while at the same time scalable enough to be adapted to a panoply of unrelated aspects, such as a particular environment, geography, demographics, a series of events, aesthetics, socio-economic class, ethnicity, volume, patterns, sensorial stimulus, function, landscape, morphology, meaning, typology, texture, choice etc. (Figure 9.1).

While diventity is about diversity, it should not be thought of as 'something between homogeneity and heterogeneity', mainly because these are states, while diventity is a quality. Homogeneity can express identity, but that identity is rarely more than the sum of its parts, and

Figure 9.1
Diventity in the architectural chaos of Beirut: the character of Wardiyeh Square in Hamra comes from the catalogue of buildings that bound it. One from each period or style: 1920s French Colonial to 1990s generic, passing through 1950s Corbusian pilotis, a Niemeyeresque church from the 1960s and a 1970s brutalist concrete shell ... The extreme variety of the volumes and lines of composition makes it almost too chaotic, but it could be simplified by reducing the visual clutter added by electricity lines for example.

therefore is not emergent but self-perpetuating. Heterogeneity has more chance of expressing emergent identity, but also risks being little more than the superposition of different clashing identities that fail to compose a larger identity. Five random consonants will have little chance of creating a meaningful word, but five random letters including vowels might come closer.

In both cases, when a homogeneous or a heterogeneous system develops the potential for an emergent identity that can then be sustained and that can interact with a larger number of emergent identities, then that system has diventity. The new emergent identity can then be related to other diverse identities to define an extra layer of diventity, and so on: random words can potentially create a meaningful sentence if, and only if, they are themselves a combination of nouns and verbs.

The diverse notes that make up the music sheet for a guitar create an emergent identity: the guitar track. This emergent identity then is confronted to the tracks of the bass, the drums, the horns, and the voice of the singer, and together they form a new emergent identity: the song. If the product of a music band is recognizable as a song, then that band has diventity. A symphony is the emergent identity of a composition with diventity. A composition without diventity produces a cacophony that cannot be recognized as 'music'.

The European Union is a new identity emerging from the diverse identities of its constituent nations: it has diventity that it is trying to sustain. The former Yugoslavia was based on an ethnic and cultural diventity that was difficult to sustain, so the system blew apart into its constituents. Similarly, Lebanon has had uneven successes with its confessional diventity (eighteen different confessions on 10 000 square kilometres), yet that is what came to give it its national identity, while its geographic diventity (a highly diverse topography and ecosystem on the same 10 000 square kilometres) gave it a territorial identity unique in the Middle East.

A jungle is a system with diventity based on a certain density of diverse species that make up its fauna and flora; it is precisely that density and diversity that differentiates it from a forest. An ecosystem can only thrive if it has diventity; an economic system cannot function without a dense presence of diverse capitals. While many small towns or suburbia might look or feel the same, it is rare for two major cities to have similar identities.

We can think of a hundred more examples of diventity at work, but in all these cases we should not forget that the concept of identity, and hence of diventity, is directly linked to the human mind's need to recognize patterns and categorize differences. Diventity requires the identity that emerges from the system to be recognized by the human mind; that is why diventity has no use outside the SST continuum's triple dimensions, and that is how it can be used as a potent concept in the definition of urban space in the post-Cartesian paradigm. Armed with this wonderful new construct, this quality *with* a name,* we can now propose our generic 'axiom for good urban space':

*Compare to Christopher Alexander's 'quality without a name'.[12]

Good urban space optimizes diventity.

This deceivingly simple axiom holds many layers of implications to the built form, especially if we keep in mind the manifold connotations of diventity and its relation to the human user's consciousness and the SST continuum, and the concept of emergent arousal and identity from a potential interference field. The following pages will attempt to formulate some of these implications and, I insist, not in the form of guidelines but in the form of potential interpretations, many of which are already present in most current urban theory: the aim here is to show how they are embraced by the quantum metaphor.

Oscillating construction blocks: life in quantum lego-land

Now that we have defined our field of play as the society–space–time continuum filled with its quantum potentiality waves, we need to furnish and shape it with some interactive elements to create urban spaces with diventity.

We are used to thinking of the main construction block of the urban realm as being the building (or any physical construction). In the quantum city the building is a duality, and a potential complementary part of a higher order duality: a building is stones~function or form~meaning (a monument or public sculpture, for example, has meaning *instead* of function), and it is part of the building~block, or building~neighbourhood (or mass~void, etc.). Each complementary of these higher order dualities is itself part of its own higher order duality, and so on. For example, the neighbourhood is part of the neighbourhood~city, the city is part of the city~conurbation or city~state, then state~nation, and so on.

In the SST continuum, human individuals are as seminal a construction unit of the urban realm as are their artefacts. The individual is another duality in itself and part of higher order dualities: body~soul, and part of individual~community, individual~family, individual~society, and so on.

A third and equally important construction unit is the natural element as used in landscaping: trees, plants, vegetation, water elements, and other composition units that are usually the field of the landscape architect, in addition to elements of the natural landscape in general. Living natural elements have the important role of acting as transitional elements between the human individual and the physical building, through a set of intrinsic qualities that will be discussed further below.

We shall refer to the three main types of construction blocks as the *human*, the *artificial* (used here without any pejorative connotations: in that sense a bird's nest is as artificial as a building made by a human) and the *natural* 'oscillators'. The role of urban design* is to lay out the construction blocks in a way that optimizes the interference patterns *within* each type, *between* the types, and between the elements and each and all of their complementary units.

*'Urban design' will refer to the product of the generic urban design unit that would optimally be the quantum urban design team described in pp. 127–131, including notably a landscape architect and a sociologist, and allowing for future manipulation by lay users.

A first level duality can be described as an oscillating particle. It is defined by its size, shape and relative position in the society–space–time field, and the different waves it emits. Each of these waves is defined by its intensity, frequency, and its event horizon's extension in each of the three dimensions: societal, spatial, and temporal.

An example of an event horizon is the perimeter from which an object is visible: the waves of an object whose experience relies on visual contact (aesthetic value, colour, form, size ...) are limited by the same rules as optical physics (diffraction, refraction, and reflection ...). Interference patterns between two such objects are created only if the concerned sources are simultaneously visible from the point of observation. Another example is event horizons that are mostly societal, i.e. perceived only by some societies and/or individuals. This is the case for 'meaning' waves, such as those associated with a memorial, for example, or a childhood memory connected to a particular place. Temporal event horizons could include those associated with periodic or even one-off events, such as seasonal festivals or weekend markets, or world fairs occupying a particular place. Legislative event horizons include street and area demarcations, zoning, and jurisdictions. One highly representative example of a legislative event horizon taking literal physical form is the building envelope such as the Hausmannian *gabarit* or the 1916 Manhattan Zoning Law, which creates theoretical ethereal volumes until the commercial and development opportunities realize those volumes into skyscrapers.

In summary, each construction unit in the SST continuum has the following basic properties:

1. It is itself a duality
2. It is part of a higher order duality
3. Its complementary is a duality
4. Its 'particle' aspect provides a visible, physical entity with variable measurable shape and mobility
5. Its 'wave' aspect provides an information field with a characteristic frequency, intensity, and an event horizon, variable in the society–space–time context.

Two or more dualities obey the following simple rules:

1. Their physical 'particle' aspects group through:
   - *juxtaposition* (next to each other)
   - *superposition* (on top of each other)
   - *opposition* (facing each other)
   - *interposition* (between two or inside one other)
   - *hyperposition* (coincide in Space but not necessarily in Time or in Society)
   - *cyberposition* (positioned in a way that there is no direct relation between their particle components, but their waves can overlap and/or interfere with the particle sources).
2. When the relative position of dualities permits their event horizons to intersect, their 'wave' aspects:
   - interfere through *constructive interference*, where the resulting wave has a greater intensity than its parent waves (extreme case is called *resonance*)
   - interfere through *destructive interference*, where the resulting wave has a lower intensity than its parent waves (extreme case is *annihilation*)
   - *do not interfere* – in some cases where the waves are quali-

tatively independent, or others where the actual interference is not cognizable by a human observer.

Any design should be based on a quantum analysis of the site, locating the major primary oscillators and their event horizons, detecting composite sources and waves, and extrapolating from interference waves the propensity of change at each point of the SST field.

Composition rules

To verify the axiom we set up, the composition of the construction blocks should comply with the following rules:

1. Since the most crucial element for the cognition of the urban design realm is the human observer, the observer's relative position is a most important composition tool. Hence the moving user's cone of vision, auditory and olfactory horizons are of prime importance.
2. It follows from rule (1) that any 'source' unit should be positioned in such a way that its 'wave' field can eventually be perceived and shared by a maximum number of observers in general, or by a regulated number in particular as in the case of private development.
3. A user (observer) can be either inside a source or outside it. Mostly, the first case represents a user inside a building, using its functions. The second case represents a user in the open space, street, square, park, etc. Therefore enough open space should be provided for observers to move in and observe from – in other words, to interfere in. Too little open space stifles the effect of a wave pattern and of diventity, and too much dilutes it.
4. Any composition follows the rules of particle grouping and wave interaction described above, and results in composite sources and interference waves.
5. Excessive monothematic grouping should be avoided as it simply amplifies or annihilates one particular wave, and reduces qualitative diversity and hence diventity.

6. Composite sources are a group of unitary sources. Even if such a group verifies rule (5) above, a repetition of it must also verify the rule of non-monothematic repetition of the composite waves.

Time and the user as an observer–designer

The insistence on the individual as a basic construction block is primary because of the individual's intrinsic role in the realization of the environment. In the same vein as the proverbial tree falling in the woods, a building or a street without a human observer is conceptually *unreal*. In that sense, it is similar to the 'Copenhagen Interpretation' of quantum theory. Since diventity is in direct connection to the information gathered by an observer, then we can postulate with our axiom that 'diventity should be available to all observers'. This of course relates directly to the quantum notion of observer/observed linkage, or the 'creative dialogue' between object and subject, man and context, with related issues of ecology and holism.

In practice, it means that all environments should be designed from the point of view (whether sensorial or conceptual) of *the user moving in the space*, and not only from that of the *professional looking from above*; that includes 'fifth elevation' cases where observers can overlook rooftops and therefore their point of view becomes a design consideration too. This in turn brings up the difference between the experience of a place in plan or in reality (Figure 9.2).

> In plan the settlement looks irregular because it lacks the formal, geometric properties we normally associate with order. Yet as a place to walk about and experience, it seems to possess order of another, more subtle, more intricate kind. The very irregularity of the ways with which the buildings aggregate appears somehow to give the hamlet a certain recognizability and suggest a certain underlying order.[13]

At the opposite end are the modernist ordered schemes, and other utopian designs, highly legible and ordered in plan, but providing dead, anonymous and disorienting environments for their user/observer (Figure 9.3). One reason for this is of course the different planning approaches, which oppose a place grown in time to an imposed bureaucratic system that needs maximum efficiency to function (grids,

Figure 9.2
Orienting disorder, or simply oriental order?

Figure 9.3
Disorienting order, in a new town/suburbia in Holland.

repetitions, and other mass production ...); many decisions guided almost purely by economical or ideological constraints have created urban environments where society, space and time and hence man, his built and natural landscapes, were woefully dislocated.

Another implication of the role of the user as observer–designer as well as being a design element comes from the need for social and temporal diventity as expressed through its human dimension. Time is at the essence of human existence and sensibility, and a need for temporal diventity produces two related yet distinct requirements. In its most literal application to human beings, temporal diventity requires the mixing of people of all age groups, young and old, children and adults, with different mobility and perception, different territories and different functional needs. This implies, amongst other things, a large variety of functions that encourage this mixing, as well as, on a smaller scale, the adaptation of the environment to the different mobility and perceptual needs – from handicapped-friendly circulation to safe children play networks, and from large and easily readable signage to attention to detail that can only be appropriated by children ...

The less direct translation of temporal diventity to humans is through the concept of relative *durée*; in other words the subjective perception of the speed of passing time. The popular reactions that 'time flies when you're having fun' or 'drags when you're bored' should be taken literally in the design of urban space that allows for mood and activity changes to create such different time perceptions. Entertainment, work, rest and cultural areas provide different moods, and hence temporal diventity, thus lending support to the need for mixed-use development. Similarly, *durée* is affected by familiarity with the space,[14] as is seen by the different temporal perceptions that, for example, a local inhabitant and a tourist have for the same environment. This implies the need to address activities and options sensitive to the different types of users: locals, visitors, tourists, short-, medium- and long-term renters, different ownership patterns, and so on.

The need for a diversity of moods, combined with one of form and uses, means urban space need not always be perfect for everyone. In fact, it almost requires that urban space makes some people less comfortable and less happy than others. Of course that should not be 'designed' or targeted towards any particular group, but one should avoid trying to please every single user, as this will only create lowest common denominator environments with little excitement. Environments should be responsive, but should also allow users to respond back, and that response includes not liking those environments. This creates a come-and-go dynamic that is necessary to the periodic human exchange between environments (with its associated cross-fertilization through memory and culture) – in other words, is at the heart of the concept of open systems essential to self-regulation.

The public–private continuum: territoriality, admissibility and the human gaze

The need to differentiate between the architect and the urban designer parallels the separation between the 'private' and the 'public' realms in Western frameworks. This of course translates into excessive atomization and hierarchization of urban space. The need conceptually as well as administratively to separate the two realms has created exclusionist territories that in turn raise issues of control, borders and security. We have created the need to separate administratively, and from it the need to separate physically and, eventually, socially. Yet if the original conceptual separation wasn't there, the end problems could be solved differently, as in the SST continuum. Here again a simple lesson can be learned from non-Western fabrics. Middle-Eastern, particularly Mediterranean, towns still reflect in some parts the conceptual continuity between private and public.

Villages, or even traditional pockets within the urban fabric of some Arabic cities, treat urban open space as a continuum that gradually moves from public to private. Unlike the sudden public/private split of modern planning, one cannot immediately feel a physical border between the totally public and the totally private domain. Here there is no need for fences or secure gates, 'keep out' or 'beware of dog' signs: the territory is marked by psychological and perceptual rather

Figure 9.4
Segregated, mechanical delineation. Signs and fences define territoriality in an estate in London.

Figure 9.5
Organic, psychological delineation. Human perception and sensitivity define admissibility in a 'rural pocket' in Beirut.

than physical moments (Figures 9.4, 9.5). Open space flows organically between fuzzy zones that rely on pedestrians' sensitivity to direct them. The immediate relationship between the architecture itself and the outside space, in other words between the inner and the outer sanctums of urban life, is sufficient to charge space with various degrees of admissibility.

The space diagram seems made of overlapping regions rather than separate zones. The overlap areas are spatial and psychological thresholds where one takes the decision to transgress the next region or not. Like a quantum system requiring only finite thresholds of energy before shifting states, territory shifts from public to private thanks to a series of different perceptual elements – a change of 'atmosphere', a presence, the sound of TV or of someone doing the dishes behind an open door, the sight of drying clothes, flower pots or a caged bird (Figure 9.6) ...

The same region can thus always be accessible but have different degrees of admissibility or welcome at different times of the day or to different people. The territoriality remains intact: for the inhabitants of such a space an intruder is immediately recognized, either because the intruder is not identified as a member of the community, or simply because of behavioural patterns. Here one's body language becomes a clue to one's identity – hesitancy, as someone who has lost his or her way, or inquisitiveness, as someone looking for the house of a friend ... in reaction, the inhabitants either adopt an indifferent, a welcoming or an alarmed curiosity, and our intruder is cued as to the next move. In the absence of people, the windows and doors that open towards the accessible space, combined with the spatial pattern generally unfamiliar to strangers, discourages trespassers: this is a safe-by-design fabric.

A similar re-integration of the other's gaze as a territorial design element is recognizable in recent urban design literature[10,15] as the 'eyes on the street' concept for creating a sense of neighbourhood watch, and hence safety. This had already been used to a more determined effect by J. B. A. Godin in his 1859 *Familistère*. Godin had made a fortune manufacturing space heaters, and had developed a strong, almost extremist, social and moral vision that he published as a manifesto in *Solutions Sociales* and in the leftist paper of *l'Association Ouvrière*. His utopian vision was put to practical experiment in the housing complex that he built for the workers of his furnace factory. The Familistère was strongly based on Charles Fourrier's Phalanstère model, but was more successful than its predecessor in creating an integrated, multi-use neighbourhood with living, shopping, education and entertainment facilities designed with strong social ideology as a support. A simple example was the introvert design of the three main housing units; each was a multi-storey quadrangle with external corridors/balconies linking the different apartments, and overlooking the inner covered courtyard and each other. With this configuration, behav-

Figure 9.6
Territoriality marked by signs of life and care: a regularly attended neighbourhood shrine.

iour inside the public space of each quadrangle was regulated through the pressure of the neighbours' gaze. It was a literal replacement for policing the Familistère, in recognition of the self-regulating ability of social units. Offenders were publicly denounced through posters and fined for their lawlessness, which varied from hanging clothes to dry on the public side of their balconies to peeing in the courtyard ...

Landscape-based design exemplifies the society–space–time unity

> Time is the Greatest innovator
> (Francis Bacon)

There is a clear relationship between the three seminal construction units and the SST continuum. While all have inherent societal, spatial and temporal dimensions to different extents, each unit can claim to represent some dimensions more than others. The artificial unit represents space, the human represents society, and the natural unit represents time (see Table 9.1).

Table 9.1
Relation between the three main oscillators and the three dimensions of the society–space–time continuum (bold crosses signify the most characteristic dimension)

Oscillator\Dim	Society	Space	Time
Human	**X**	X	X
Artificial	X	**X**	
Natural		X	**X**

Humans are social entities that change in time and in space: they move around and grow in size and in age. They relate to each other and to their environment through their memory and their perception of the passing of time.

While artificial entities do change in time in form, size and/or function, even as they retain a rather fixed position in space, they do so at a rate that is normally too slow for the human user to appreciate.

Natural entities, in contrast, change in time at a more perceptible rate. They change colour, size, shape and texture in short, periodic spans, yet frequently outlive even artificial structures. Throughout the seasons they provide the human observer with visual, olfactory and even aural (wind through the leaves, singing birds and crickets …) signals of the periodic passing of time.

By sharing their limited mobility and their space-forming properties with those of artificial entities, and their 'alive-ness' with humans, natural elements constitute a perfect link between man and his built environment across society–space–time. In fact, this reading of the role of nature as a mending element, through the human need for a sense of time (in other words, of a sense of history) might provide a new explanation for the preference of many users for so-called 'traditional' environments.

Seeing that preference as one for places with an embedded history and sense of time provides a new clue towards the design of better urban space: without the need for a copying of past forms, or even past configurations, it becomes possible for the designer to incorporate this sense of time through the early adoption of landscape-based plans. In turn, well-designed landscape-based schemes tend to have high ecological value and sustainable qualities, conceptually linking back to the holistic, ecological quantum worldview. In terms of educational and professional practice, the necessity of the landscape architect as an integral part of the urban design team, and the necessity of a better focus on the integration of landscape-related studies into the curriculum of architecture and urban design courses, becomes clearer.

Looked at from another point of view, this time using the concept of diventity as applied to the added diversity of forms, colours, textures, smells and periodicities that natural elements provide, as well as the added diversity of ecosystems and eventually of living species, the same necessity for natural elements reappears as an essential extra layer of information that can easily become much more exciting than, for example, superfluous ornamentation.

Built form as memory storage media or the city as memorial

In Hebrew, as in Arabic, man (*zakar* or *zekher*) and memory (*zakira*) have the same root. In addition, the Arabic language also uses *zakira* to signify the navel: the central point (a spatial dimension), but also the tip of the umbilical cord that connects mother and child (a social dimension). Man is memory, and memory is an absolute necessity in his continuous connection with himself, his life and his temporal dimension (Figure 9.7).

Traditional environments tend to provide two main aspects linked to time. One is related to meaning and a cultural value system that recognizes in such environments a historical importance, and hence a temporal dimension to be sustained. The second can be more simply

Figure 9.7
Old man reminiscing under the last tree standing in what is left of Martyrs Square, once the heart of the Beirut city centre, after bulldozers razed it in 1993.

visual, and can be related to the generally denser style or patterning of traditional architecture that links back to the density of the information field and arousal levels, and hence to the recognition of identity–diventity. From a slightly more subtle point of view, it might be again related to an unconscious human affinity to the time invested in the designing and manufacturing of such buildings, say through the attention to detail or the hand-sculpted ornamentation, or even the brick-by-brick construction by human hands. It is as if the affinity is not towards the building itself but towards those who built it, as the building becomes simply the storage medium of the message the original builders were sending out to their successors. Again, this is similar to the affinity many contemporary architects (as opposed to laypeople in general) feel for the intellectual feats of the designers of Modern buildings: humans invariably need to feel this connection (or confrontation) with their historical peers.

Therefore there are three types of memory that built form should tackle: the subjective memory related to meaning, and directly linked to each individual's sense of personal and group identity (*zakira* – memories); the collective memory of preceding civilizations or even close ancestors (*zakira* – umbilical cord); and the memory of the knowledge and worldview of the designers and builders (*zakira* – navel of the world). Each one of these memories implies different effects to built form, so some examples are given below.

Subjective memory

New built form should not force any particular non-contemporary 'style' on coming generations, but rather respect their own capacity of adding meaning layers to whatever is built today, which means new built form should have a wide range of adaptability, both physical and aesthetical. On the other hand, existing built form should be judged according to the same rule – in other words, even settings with no immediate architectural or historical value should be respected, saved and/or upgraded, if found to have particular meanings attached to their current users. In particular, attention should be given to the layers of meaning children have added to the environment, as in most cases these would be the most subtle, and the ones with most lifespan ahead.

Collective memory

Existing built form of particular historical value, as linked to cultural and/or national identity, should be safeguarded without falling into the excesses of some forms of critical regionalism in terms of over-emphasis on particular moments in history at the expense of a longer historical continuum. An example is some ex-colonial cities, such as Beirut, which finds its architectural heritage of the 1940s to 1970s totally unattended, although it provides some excellent examples of Modernist buildings. At the same time pre-twentieth century houses have all but disappeared, while the late Ottoman and French mandate architecture is the only layer being protected – and even then with uneven success. This creates discontinuity in the layers of history of the city, and adds to the risk of isolating and fetishizing fragments rather than integrating them in the overall fabric.

Knowledge memory

Since built form should archive the knowledge of its builders, it becomes the whole civilization's legacy to its successors. As such, it should be continuously up to date – in other words, strictly contemporaneous to its SST context. This translates into technological aspects, construction and form, socio-economic structure and cultural aspects. It should archive our current quantum worldview in all its aspects: relational, holistic, ecological, technological, spiritual, indeterminist, complementary, etc. Just like the pyramids of Egypt, a great recent example is the Bilbao Guggenheim museum and its relationship to the city. Frank Gehry's masterpiece archives the extraordinary technological achievements of the digital age, as its formal complexity would have been impossible to build without the use of CAD and computerized manufacturing processes, even a few years earlier.

Aesthetically it embodies the formal freedom and tolerance of its time, and functionally it houses cultural artefacts of its present. Its effect on Bilbao has been more than simply spatial, creating a non-local shockwave that put it on the international map of architectural destinations, and provided the city with an emblem, a similar feat to, say, the Eiffel Tower in Paris. This in turn conveys additional information on the socio-economic system of international tourism that upholds such a bravura gesture. All these layers of information will be recovered one day by the archeologists of the fifth millennium; it is with such a prospect in mind that major urban interventions should be approached.

The respect of these three memories creates a diverse environment on many scales: from the non-local diversification of international experiences down to the multi-layered diventity of historical and architectural strata, and further down to architectural and/or tectonic expression that can chose any level of expression of its technological processes (including context-sensitive and bio-climatic design) as long as it is up to date and updatable. This is automatically regulated by its inclusion of ecological and sustainability issues, resulting from cultural values inherent in the techno-spiritual quantum worldview.

Awareness before construction

Diventity is mostly an issue of human consciousness being aware and sensitive to a set of information, thanks to an optimal level of arousal that information triggers in the sensory register and the mind of an observer. Too little arousal means too little information, and too much information means too much clutter; both cases reduce receptivity to diventity. In the quantum worldview where the physical and the mental are interchangeable, this means that the way to heightened diventity is not always about new construction: sometimes all a 'bad' urban space needs to become 'good' is clarification of the information field it offers. We must not forget that extreme density of diversity is negative, as it overloads the sensory system with information. Therefore a reduction of information clutter is sometimes a possible path to regeneration. In turn this does not necessarily mean clearing of excessive *objects* in the urban realm, but rather the reduction of the number of different identities of the same level by grouping them into higher order identities: a simple, straightforward example would be unifying the colour scheme of a street or neighbourhood if the architectural and spatial experience is too overwhelming – sometimes a simple coat of paint will do.

The opposite works well too; for example, if the architectural and spatial experience is not arousing enough, simple differentiation with colour and new personalization elements can boost the diventity by creating an extra scale of identities. For instance, in some streets of Dublin colorizing the individual house facades has enlivened terraced houses of otherwise monolithic brick.

Another approach is due to the fact that, in the SST continuum, the human user is as much a construction unit as are the artificial or the natural oscillators, and therefore it is possible for the urban designer to intervene directly on the users to better the interface with their environment. Do not worry; I am not talking about any form of genetic engineering; it is simply a matter of doing what public relations professionals or even tourism authorities do – raising awareness using the means available to any publicist or advertiser or newsmaker: if users can be made to consume one brand more than the other, then they can similarly be made to see the potentialities and positive aspects of their own environment. This additional awareness of the 'potential of the place' has many implications: combined with the right policy measures and partnership incentives it empowers the users to affect change (which in turn requires that the users be made aware of their own rights and potential); it creates a better identification between the users and their environment and can lead to them taking better care of it themselves. This ranges from small physical interventions (a flower pot here, a painted wall there) to economic investments (opening a flower shop, sponsoring a street art festival) ... which in turn add up to a better expression of the identity of the place (Figure 9.8).

Thanks to the equivalence between potential energy and matter, between *culture* and *form*, urban design can provide solutions not

Figure 9.8
An example where laissez-faire was put to a positive use, allowing a student to intervene positively in public space without waiting for governmental authorization. The dispossessed children of the Palestinian refugee camp of Chatila used to play on this rough concrete stairwell top as if it were a slide. An architecture student from the American University of Beirut clad it with smooth metal plates, and installed handrails and a ladder, transforming it into a 'proper' giant slide. The children absolutely loved it, and the event has triggered interest in the area. A few months later, an ad hoc playground was created around the slide within the limited resources of the community.

necessarily based on physical construction, but on events and awareness of events. Less costly, more creative interventions can be considered.

Surfaces and textures as wave sources and relays

When designing within a fixed overall morphological framework (which
is most often the case), the same rule of the observer's sensory point
of view still applies, as the focus becomes smaller scale detailing and
differentiation of experiences.

The play of light and shadow and the different effects on the sense of
touch make varied texture a major arousal-generating source. This
allows texture to break away from its typical reduction to 'traditional'
or hand-made architecture, leaving that aspect of its importance to be
tackled by the concept of affinity to 'invested time' discussed above.
Modern technology and construction materials can now reclaim the use
of texture to add to the visual and sensorial diventity, while at the same
time showing off their capacity to produce texture mechanically without
any apologetics.

Salingaros proposes *texture* as an information-generating source, and
insists on it being the reason why 'traditional' architecture contains
more information. Hence the excuse to claim the uncritical superiority
of traditional architecture as urban space boundary. However, in claiming so he denies some wonderful properties of materials he considers
anathema for his information field; glass and other polished stone and
marble. Their very reflectivity can be an information source, relaying
visual cues, hints of happenings from a place otherwise inaccessible
to the observer. At the same time, he seems to forget that the needed
texture does not have to be supplied exclusively by 'artificial' elements.
Natural elements easily complement any urban composition with their
living texture, as we have discussed above.

The authors of *Responsive Environments*[10] address the issue with the
quality of 'richness' through visual cues. Their adoption of a visual

richness composition rule variable according to the 'likely range of distances from which the surface concerned will be viewed' is similar to the definition of the visual event horizon (Figure 9.9). By adding the second factor, 'the length of time during which the surface concerned will be viewed', they effectively add a temporal dimension to the visual event horizon; finally, they hint at the social dimension of the society–space–time continuum in the chapter on 'visual appropriateness'. They provide examples of visual richness based on texture and shadows, and even suggest that sustained visual richness could be achieved through visual riddles and interpretation. Unfortunately, their illustrations are biased towards European small towns and traditional buildings and stonework, and thus produce a reductive (albeit seductive to many) image of what richness could be in the twenty-first century.

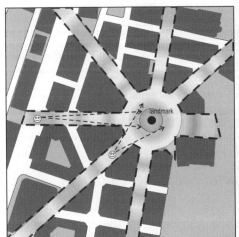

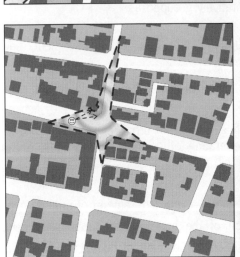

Figure 9.9
The visual event horizon. Plan and reality.

Figure 9.10
Magic in the urban realm:
Nouvel's Cartier Foundation, Bvd
Raspail, Paris.

In reality, not all settings even contain traditional architecture. A careful introduction of a variety of textures and styles, even the most contrasting, provides contemporaneity (thus *making sense* to current and future users) and, if artfully implemented, can produce a touch of pure magic in the urban realm. A masterful example is Jean Nouvel's Cartier Foundation building in Paris, an incredible high-tech building that uses transparency and reflection of natural elements to integrate itself in its Hausmannian surroundings (Figure 9.10).

Initial states in new large-scale development

When starting a new large-scale development, different main scenarios present themselves, tentatively grouped as:

A   Development in a natural setting (greenfield development, new towns ...)

B   Development over artificial reclaimed land (sea front reclamation, *tabula rasa* ...)

C   Development over existing land in an urban environment (brownfield development, regeneration of de-industrialized sites, urban renewal schemes ...)

Each of these categories presents a very different set of original interference patterns, and hence of the states of the potentiality field, broadly related to the presence or absence of human, artificial and natural oscillators. Table 9.2 shows a simplified interpretation of this relation.

Main oscillators (development type)	Human (society)	Artificial (space)	Natural (time)
A natural setting	none	none	yes
B *tabula rasa*	**none**	**none**	**none**
C regeneration	yes	yes	none
'good urban space'	**yes**	**yes**	**yes**

Table 9.2 Main oscillators at initial state of three main development types. Note: negligible oscillation is simplified as none

It is easy to see from Table 9.2 how different the three pre-design analyses should be. In particular, it shows how much more difficult it is to create 'good' urban space that addresses all three urban dimensions starting from a *tabula rasa*, as most modern urbanism has proved. The variety and intensity of potential is already higher in type C than in types A and B, suggesting a more sensible approach to regeneration than immediate razing and re-development, and linking back to the landscape-based regeneration issues mentioned above. It also proves that densification rather than extension over greenfield areas would require less effort and expense than imagined, even on the short and mid terms.

Importantly, it also shows the difference between a *tabula rasa* and a natural setting, which incorporates at least a temporal dimension, and a minimum propensity field, hence suggesting a design approach consciously respectful of the meanings and roles of the different natural oscillators in greenfield development. Chinese and oriental planners continue to heed the importance of natural elements as life-force (*chi*) sources and deflectors, and successfully use the science of feng shui, which is about the recognition of the propensity field's patterns and their interference, for the settlement of their new towns;[16] the quantum metaphor allows Western planning to break away from its objective pride and simulate sensitivity to such 'quaint' matters.

Transition phases: colonizing the vacuum

In the quantum metaphor, human users perceive their environment through the interference of the oscillations of different sources. According to the quantum analysis of the urban realm, interference patterns produce observable new states at discrete, discontinuous intervals, inversely proportional to the amount of change introduced.

Such intervals sometimes stretch over considerable periods of time, as in the case of post-war reconstruction, for example, or in any large-scale development. Although phasing is accounted for in most of these cases, designers and architects tend to look at these prolonged transition periods as simple construction phases.

In reality these represent particular states of the environment, during which the interference patterns of the system are very different from the original state at which the design was produced, and from which the final, built state is also quite different.

This explains why most traditional cities give out the impression of unity and continuity. Their piecemeal growth in time meant that every single new building added responded to the exact interference patterns of the moment; every additional intervention responded to a natural realization of a potentiality reaching its maturity. This response to the correct contemporaneous state of the system keeps transitional periods and the quantum jumps to a minimum. It creates an integrity that is extremely difficult to replicate with large-scale development, which leaves huge gaps in both time and space.

Christopher Alexander and his students have approached a similar effect through their 'New Theory of Urban Design', where they produced a city quarter following a simple set of rules, the most important of which is the insistence on the *exact moment* of each new building as the main design context:

> ... the *timing* of a vision, ... the way that the 'next' project always depends, for its details, on the moment in time sequence when it is first imagined.

[...] the proposal should be enormously sensitive to the *exact* moment in sequence when it comes ... a certain proposal might make sense as P_n if it comes after P_{n-1}, but as soon as even one other proposal comes in between, *even in a place fairly far away from that location*, then a properly executed project at the same place where P_n was will have to be enormously different from P_n. [...] it is even possible that the whole idea [function] of what is proposed [next] might no longer be relevant at all – because as a result of [the previous addition], the gestalt of the whole has shifted so enormously.[17]

From the moment site preparation begins to the final occupancy stage, the growing of the project as well as the adaptation of its setting to its existence – or rather, to the disappearance of whatever sources it replaced in the first place – would have produced new interferences – potentialities and choices unimagined at the design stage.

Design typically is based on the analysis of a context fixed in time at the moment the analysis itself is made. Even projected estimates of the contextual situation at the time of completion are more often than not based on statistical data that can never account for the complexity and uncertainty of the social–space–time continuum. For this reason, no large-scale design project should be finished on paper as long as construction evolves. Even when the issue of *robustness*[10] is tackled as a design quality, the objective should be to provide *adaptability and variability at the stage of the design and construction process itself*, and not only at that of the finished building: designing a generic building and hoping that it will adapt easily after it is completed is not the way to do it.

The notion of spatial and temporal discontinuity created by large-scale development ('Bigness' in Rem Koolhas's categorization) links back to the states of *tabula rasa* development of the previous paragraph; the transition period covering site acquisition, clearance, design, planning permission, construction, up to occupancy leaves a large site inaccessible to the user/observer for a long time, effectively producing a discontinuity in the urban realm in all three of its main dimensions. An extreme case of both *tabula rasa* and large-scale development is postwar reconstruction.

Ruins as primary wave sources and other development seeds

Tabula rasa sites provide, just as their name implies, a totally clear field that includes a 'wave silence', as there are no sources to provide the basic interference patterns the human mind picks up as information.

This is extremely important when dealing with post-war reconstruction, where in most cases the *tabula rasa* results from a total bulldozing of whatever ruins were left. It is the typical approach of most reconstruction policies that a combination of political and economical agendas push for a complete erasure of the remnants of a painful conflict.

By doing so, it leaves a gaping hole in the historical development of the place and breaks it away from people's collective memory. Even if the new design borrows on past forms or uses exact reproduction, developing from scratch always leaves strong discrepancies in the society–space–time continuum. As the French symbolist, philosopher and playwright Alfred Jarry wrote in the last century, 'You won't have destroyed everything until you have destroyed the ruins'.

An extreme example, again from Beirut, is the destruction marks left on the built form during fifteen years of little wars. To a whole generation that ruined environment, or those wild-growth infested, bullet-ridden buildings, have constituted the setting of their childhood. Post-war political reconstruction generally fears trauma; hence it requires amnesia, and therefore all traces of destruction are erased, and with it the support of the collective memory of a generation. When even recent memory is given its fair value, and a minimum of traces are kept, then all generations are respected and better social, spatial and temporal cohesion can be achieved in the long term.

Even if a building has been bombed, and deserted by its human inhabitants, it retains reverberations of their past presence. Present in the very stones of a ruin, they disappear with its total removal, but their effect can be relayed by the new design. In that sense, the memory of the place, considered in the quantum environment as an intrinsic aspect of any man-made environment, should be respected and addressed as a design object equal in importance to any tangible physical object: if the destruction of the ruins is inevitable, then Jarry's worry can be addressed by at least keeping a memory of the *destruction* of the ruins itself. That memory can be kept in a multitude of ways, from memorials to archives or museums, but also through the recognition of the waves left behind even in the absence of the original physical structure: a very Zen-like sensibility to the presence of absence takes over.

Economically based site clearing in post-war development should therefore be checked by the appreciation of the meaning and value of the ruins themselves: wherever possible, traces of the original buildings should be kept and used as starting oscillation sources from which to build up the new environment, as a reactive adaptation to the interferences of these primary sources. With time, as the new construction gathers momentum and solidifies its social, spatial and temporal dimensions, it is possible, if needs be, to dispose of the original ruins or to 'let them die of their natural death'.[18]

The same approach should be adapted with all large-scale development – building in phases and moving in occupants regularly and, in the case of regeneration, finishing new segments before destroying old ones, even if it entails a more delicate management of resources. People can live near damaged buildings as long as they are in a safe environment (unfortunately some even live in them out of necessity). In fact damaged and rundown buildings can provide an essential sense of time and, if ingeniously used as architectural scarecrows, can play the role of a catalyst for improvement.

One way of colonizing the vacuum or the large-scale site over the long period of construction would be by 'seeding' all of the site and then densifying gradually rather than growing out from an initial single cell or centre. This process is about scattering initial buildings or events on different points of the site in such a way that a minimal overlap of their different event horizons is still possible. Once activated, they will fill the space between them with potentiality waves that can then trigger further design response, particularly at the area of overlap that might itself create an emergent need for a new intervention. The process is then repeated as the initially empty site is first filled with potential, then densified with form. This provides a faster and more integral way of colonizing the site than the typical cluster phasing, which leaves huge areas of the site empty for too long. The difference is based on the notion that areas where event horizons overlap are not empty, but are filled with potential matter defined by energetic interferences: the concept of malleable energy fields developed in the previous chapter. In cluster phasing, empty areas are sterile. A fine example of such an approach is Christian de Portzamparc's winning urban design scheme for the Masséna district in Paris (Figure 9.11).

Figure 9.11
Secteur Masséna, C. de Portzamparc. The concept of open block, where free-standing buildings mushroom according to relationship rules with a set of fixed buildings, providing a continuously variable and dynamic composition tool.

Another example of such a growth system is the development of historical city components gradually over time, when most development was about gradual densification; in particular, traditional *souks* or the organic equivalent of commercial centres (*souks* are a more continuous version of informal street markets). *Souks* generally start with the settlement of a few points of sale close to a major commerce route or a port, where it is easy to buy goods from the wholesalers and sell it in bits to the density of people who generally flock around such areas. For example, if a butcher sets up shop near a port, selling cheap imported meat, after a short while his success will be picked up by another butcher, who will most probably install his shop close to the first but just outside the first's 'catchment area' (a series of event horizons, including distance on foot, smell of the meat, visibility, and customer loyalty) – especially as at the beginning there is still enough space for both not to have to compete directly. With time, a third butcher realizes he can install his shop between both butcheries and sell at slightly lower prices; he creates an overlap between the two initial shops, and interference and hence competition begins. A new dynamic of trade emerges; more butchers want to come into the area, each offering slightly different products, as prices cannot be taken down any further, and more and more customers start to recognize this as a new identity: the 'meat market'. Meanwhile a similar pattern is creating a 'textile market' also near the port, but just outside the territory of the 'meat market' for hygiene and status considerations; it is ready to tempt the meat buyers into becoming potential textile buyers. Ever sensitive to the needs of the new clientele, a jeweller offers gold bracelets at unbeatable prices, soon emulated by others, and a 'gold market' is born ... diventity constantly creates new identities, until eventually the identities densify and combine to create a higher order identity: the *souk*. The *souks* add up to the administrative, the residential and the entertainment territories and so on, densifying and diversifying the public realm until the new identity 'city' emerges.

Landmarks and events: local wave disturbance sources

In all cases, surprise and incongruous inevitability should always be present in an urban scheme. As much as the human mind is comfortable with familiar environments, it is capable of reinterpreting situations in the most adaptive of ways. In fact, if intelligence can be defined as the capacity to adapt to new situations, then the human mind is by definition adaptive, and requires diversity precisely for that reason.

Diversity is 'mind candy'. The realization that space makes us smarter should be used as a cue for commercial designers to stop patronizing the users by providing people with 'what they expect'.

Sometimes the potentiality patterns call on a seemingly incongruous addition or gesture, and this should be allowed to happen. The human mind will recognize the patterns that lead to the most 'surprising' of changes; it unconsciously expects and requires it, and will soon internalize it as an inevitable part of the whole. Such elements, whether formally or functionally incongruous, become landmarks that help improve the imageability and legibility of a setting, and hence play an important part in the identification with a place. Conversely, the human mind will – even unconsciously – recognize a desistance in the response to incongruity and ultimately get bored with it or fail to identify with it: to forfeit from embracing incongruity lowers diventity.

Applying the same logic to situations where interference has either neutralized all waves to a level of non-arousal or homogenized the environment away from diventity, an unexpected element with quantitatively and qualitatively different waves needs to be introduced to create a disturbance in the monotonous field. A bang with a shockwave needs be introduced. Such an event, in the language of chaos and fractals theory, would function as a 'strange attractor', eventually having major influence on the quantum environment.

In the context of a society–space–time continuum, this event by no means necessarily implies a physical building, fixed in time and space. It relates to the most generic sense of a man-made element. It includes lampposts and skyscrapers, advertisement billboards and neon signs, cultural festivals and periodic sales. It can be anything from a special leasing policy, a new function introduced, or a newly planted tree, a water fountain or a carnival.

By using the generic concept of duality, it is possible to integrate even such otherwise underestimated construction blocks into the vocabulary of the professional urban designer. By doing so, a stronger bridge can be spanned between theory and practice on one hand, and the different theoretical approaches on the other: more *Responsive Environments*[10] can be achieved by *Learning From Las Vegas.*[19]

Event horizons: an edge is not a border

In the mechanical/atomistic approach to planning and urban design, each urban design element is thought of as a single particle with one clearly limited position in time and space. In the quantum city, each event has in addition to its SST position a number of event horizons representing the effective territories of the different waves associated with it. The different event horizons of one event rarely coincide exactly in space, and even less so in society and in time. In addition, the total intertwining of the three SST dimensions makes it almost impossible to speak of one actual envelope as the boundary or frontier of an event. It could be possible to speak of a combined spatial horizon, which would be the furthermost perimeter of the overlap of all event horizons with a spatial dimension (Figure 9.12), but again, because of the impossibility of isolating any of the SST dimensions without discrediting the analysis, that combined spatial horizon cannot claim to contain within it all possible effects of an event, especially if we remember the non-local role of the human user. It flows from this logic that no event

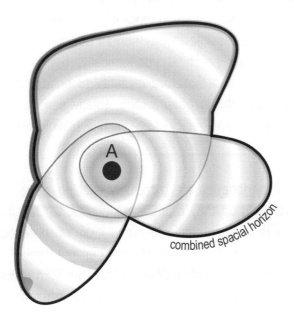

Figure 9.12
A combined spatial horizon.

combined spacial horizon

A

can be totally and absolutely separated from another, and that any event horizon is really a fuzzy envelope that can always be transcended by some other horizon.

Traditional planning and modernist zoning like to speak of edges and borders, limits and jurisdictions as if these really were impermeable envelopes. The result is either functional or socio-economic ghettos, or prioritization of centre over periphery. In the dense quantum city each periphery is always the periphery of at least two adjacent events, and is always made up of a blur of at least two sets of event horizons.

Even if we were to consider only the combined spatial horizons of two events, their exact delineation is impossible to predict with any precision (Uncertainty Principle) because a human observer with mobility and memory will be able to transcend those horizons, carrying away the consciousness of the effect of one event outside its spatial event horizon and confronting it with the effect of the other event.

It follows that the whole notion of no-man's land becomes irrelevant, unless taken literally; if two events are really to be totally independent, then the space between their spatial event horizons and the time between their temporal event horizons should be hermetically inaccessible to any human consciousness. Such a situation is rarely practical economically, but it also means reducing density and therefore diventity to unacceptable levels in the quantum city. In other words, totally separate events in the quantum city are not possible, and a minimum of overlaps is unavoidable.

Overlaps of peripheries are extremely exciting places, because when waves add up they represent a qualitative densification of diversity and a quantitative accumulation of potentiality that boost the chances for diventity. Remember that diventity is about an emergent identity that is different than the sum of its diverse component identities. That means the edge is itself the centre

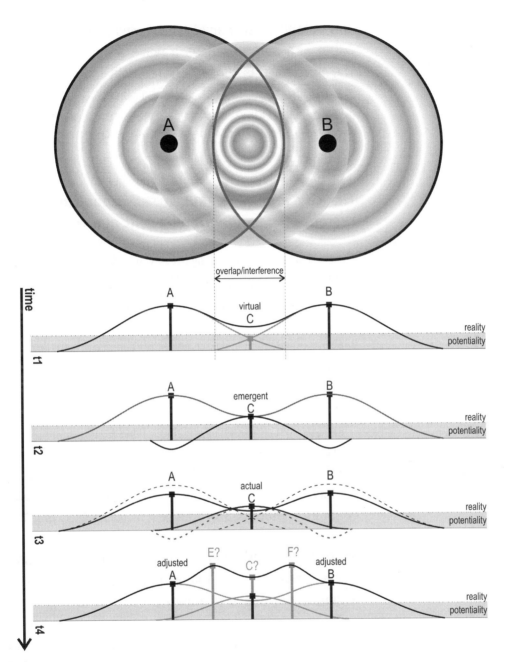

Figure 9.13
Periphery emerges as centre. The waves of events A and B overlap to produce an interference system wave at t1. The new wave raises the potentiality of event C (which is at the periphery of both A and B), making it 'jump' into reality: C emerges at time t2 as a new potential centre. If acted upon by a human, it can be activated and sustained in reality, and automatically creates its own wave. Notice the negative values of C's wave near the centre of events A and B. We can think of this as 'competition due to the relative novelty of event C'. The C wave now interferes with the original waves of A and B, leading to a new state in t3, where the effects of A and B are slightly diminished to compensate for the emergence of C, and the 'negative' effects of C have flattened out. At this point, the waves interfere together again (feedback loop), resulting in a whole new 'vibration' in t4, potentially triggering events E and F, as the potentiality wave at their position goes beyond the 'existence barrier' between potentiality and reality etc.

of a potential new identity that takes a life of its own, which will in turn spread out as a wave around that new centre. The new wave in turn interferes with the original waves of the original events, raising their diventity at some points, eventually building up into a chain reaction of events that transform the whole system (Figure 9.13).

The city and its region: a self-organizing quantum system of neighbourhoods and quarters

> I think it is not too strong to say that the challenge of pluralism, the challenge of learning to live with others who are different from ourselves and doing so in a *creative* way, is one of the greatest challenges facing social, national and international stability in our times.[20]

In the quantum metaphor every element is a duality and part of a higher order duality, which is qualitatively and quantitatively different to its two complementary aspects.

Starting with the human, natural and artificial units, the next step is community and neighbourhood and, eventually, society and city. In such a model that needs to verify the quantum metaphor's properties of tolerance, pluralism and complementarity, a city is a self-organizing quantum system of neighbourhoods and quarters. A differentiation should be made between a traditional group of neighbourhoods (Figure 9.14) and a quantum group.

In the current global context, immigration, migration and differential development have created cities inhabited by various social groups, ethnicities, income levels and lifestyles. This has resulted in two general models of a city and community composition: the melting pot, and the mosaic.

The melting pot literally dilutes the individual characteristics of each group or sub-community into one overall

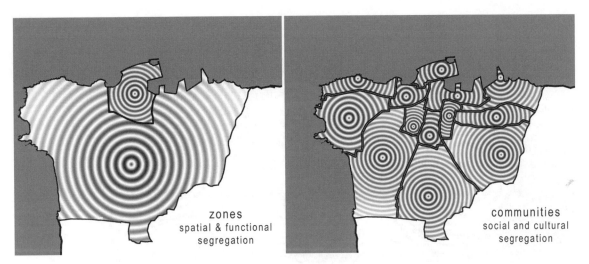

zones
spatial & functional
segregation

communities
social and cultural
segregation

Figure 9.14
The City of Zones vs. The City of Communities (after Leon Krier[22]).

colourless whole. Examples range from some American societies to globalization and the urbanism of capital.

The other extreme is the mosaic juxtaposition of identities. Usually synonymous with ghettoization and/or gentrification, it is a segregationist response to multiplicity. While such a situation usually oscillates between tolerance and conflict, it is no more than a spatial distribution of homogeneous groups in clearly entrenched quarters. No overlaps are permitted, and the result is an atomized city where any infringement of the accepted inner borders could lead to full-scale chaos. Examples include the Los Angeles heteropolis[21] and, to a certain extreme, Bosnia. A quantum city operates differently.

> In an evolving or quantum society, mere *tolerance* of the other is not enough. Both conflict and tolerance keep the other at arm's length. Both stress that he or she – the Black, the Asian, the Muslim, the Jew, [the rich, the poor] etc. – is *other* than myself. The other is no part of my experience except in so far as he or she impinges upon me. The other is no part of my identity, of my 'I-ness'. The other does not get under my skin.[20]

Applying Zohar's words to a different level shows a quantum city as a synthesis of the two responses to

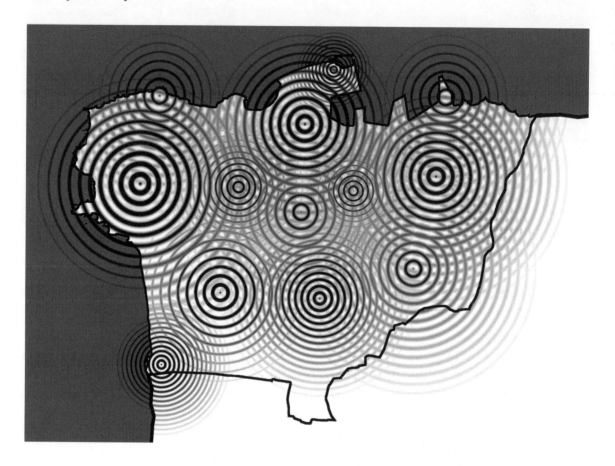

Figure 9.15
The Quantum City of Quantum Communities. Unlike Figure 9.14, the 'waves' of the different neighbourhoods overlap and interfere, creating areas of added interest.

pluralism presented above, as it accepts and respects the role and the rights of each individual group or quarter (particle) and the need for an overall (wave) identity. The result is a duality that includes all three aspects: the individual, the overall, and the individual–overall emergent identity: city-scale diventity.

Such a model implies that both cultural and formal plurality are maintained and incorporated into a new overall identity, based on mutual recognition, rather than mutual exclusion or assimilation. It is possible through the breaking down of physical borders and permitting overlaps within the overall structure. The resulting interference patterns create cultural and formal *métissage* that varies the experiences of the city, hence responding to the axiom of good urban space (Figure 9.15).

Cultural *métissage* in the quantum metaphor is not the loss of the mother cultures, but their mutual development of a new expression that belongs simultaneously to all of them. It is by no means a homogenization of cultures, but a continuous, dynamic dialogue and creation of new cultures.

Expressed architecturally, the result is not a postmodern eclectic pastiche, but a true creative and mutual reinterpretation of form. In fact, the key difference between the postmodern approach and the quantum approach is the incorporation of *meaning* as a necessary and relevant ingredient in the latter, while the former either denies meaning itself or its contextuality.

The result is, to paraphrase Zohar, a city of cities, not cities within a city. In a quantum city, each neighbourhood is functionally and spatially self-sufficient (multi-use, walkability, etc.) but also creatively interconnected with each and all other neighbourhoods. Each individual is both local and cosmopolitan, each community identity unique and shared. A quantum city has a highly vibrant potentiality field that allows a great diversity of choices of existence to its inhabitants and visitors.

Taken further, a quantum city can be read as part of a quantum agglomeration, or city region, then of a country or nation ... suggesting new ways of looking at inter-national organizations, the European Union, global cultures and so on – for example, the conceptual replacement of state or nation borders by ambiguous, overlapping fringes where qualitatively different morphologies and/or cultures could develop. This vision opens up new approaches to concepts of territoriality, cultural identity, and fringe development ...

In the sixties, architects hadn't yet thrown out the idea that two-thirds of Paris could be razed, that one could at last build a clean, hygienic, homogeneous, modern city... But the films of Antonioni and Godard were partly shot in historic cities and partly in modern neighbourhoods. This was a new, more productive way of seeing things. Whether they date from the thirties, from 1750 or from 1850, buildings are always our contemporaries. They are our coffee-pots, our tables and our chairs. We use them with the same straightforwardness. That is the strength of the city. *Time is alive there*, whereas in a museum it is embalmed. Only cities can offer us this happiness ... Cities and literary texts.
(Christian de Portzamparc[1])

We have to imagine 1001 other concepts of city.
(Rem Koolhaas[2])

transition

The incomparable scientific and technological development of the last century has transformed our culture and our lifestyles in ways we still fail to comprehend totally. Differential development has dug a deeper chasm between the First and Third Worlds, while at the same time communication technology has brought humans closer than ever. Migration and counter-migration has hybridized our cultures and our environments, and globalization is slowly homogenizing the planet.

At the threshold of the third millennium, the city is undergoing increasing stress to adapt to the new *modus operandi* of its inhabitants. Professionals of the urban realm have the role and the responsibility to think and produce – or permit the production – of environments that respond to the expectations, both conscious and unconscious, both current and future, of their users. Yet faced with unforeseen new problems and bitter past failures, urbanism seems to be at a loss of a common ground upon which to root its theories. Instead, urbanologists, from planners to designers and from architects to historians, still fall into antipodal dogmas that insist on determinist theories as fail-proof solutions to ever changing problems.

Theory and practice have splintered into many opposing camps, but most, at least in terms of declared positions, see in the Modern period the roots of all evil when it comes to designing urban space. While the Modern agenda focused on its 'now' as the sole context of its concerns, postmodern reactionary theory's main camps can be broadly grouped into traditionalists and futurists. The former looks at past traditional forms as the forgotten miracle cure for all the ailments of today's society, while the latter, like a child blinded by so many new toys, finds in the new imagery and technologies hints of a cyber-future that is bound to happen, a future where *real* urban space plays a secondary role.

In the realm of international education, students of architecture and urban design are forced to choose between two approaches; one that threatens global decontextualization – a 'flamboyant' International Style of sorts – and another that threatens excessive localism and parochialism.

In a conflictual context, this book set out to find a common denominator to use as a *background metaphor* to both education and practice; one that would permit the coexistence of opposing models that would learn from the past and still make sense to an uncertain future, and one that could accommodate change and chaos, yet sustain an evolutionary order.

Western culture, unfortunately, has developed, ever since Descartes and Newton, a worldview in which man is totally independent of his environment, where reason and feeling are totally separate, and body and soul have nothing in common. That worldview is referred to as 'the Cartesian paradigm', and has shaped most of our conceptual thought for the last few centuries.

Looking back at the historical development of city form, and charting it alongside that of scientific and philosophical thought, produces a consistent observation: most environments considered today as 'successful' have one thing in common; they did not or do not conform to a Cartesian paradigm. Many non-Western cultures continue to produce urban form that is congruent to their view of a unified universe (albeit sometimes corroded by Western-style market forces); the most celebrated examples of 'good' urban space in the Western world have been designed before the Scientific Revolution of the seventeenth century while, conversely, the worst disasters of Modern urbanism were made in the name of the 'world as a machine' paradigm ...

Contemporary knowledge provides the background to any paradigm as, by definition, a paradigm is the popularization of current beliefs. Interestingly, there seems to be a lag of two or three generations (up to 70 years) between the date of a major scientific discovery and its palpable effect on the worldview. The last half-century corresponds to this 'incubation period' of radical discoveries in science and biology: relativity theory (1905–1925), quantum theory (1930+), DNA, chaos and complexity theories (1955+) have been steadily transforming our core knowledge and our relationship with each other and the rest of the universe – our whole worldview.

The emerging worldview is dubbed 'the quantum paradigm'. It mends together body and soul, matter and mind, form and meaning. It provides powerful concepts that can be exportable outside science, and in particular to the study of the city.

Most cultures recognize the immense power of language – *in the beginning was the Word* – and therefore it was necessary to develop a semantic extension to our conceptual language. Instead of using a complicated set of 'qualities' of urban space, one simple caveat engages the human users/observers and their environment in a necessarily creative dialogue: human and environment mutually realize each other.

The implications of the new language–attitude are many. The most important implication is the interpenetration and permutation of the three dimensions of the urban realm – society, space and time – and the three constituent elements that represent them – the human, the artificial and the natural – into what we call the society–space–time (SST) continuum.

The SST construct permits – *obliges* – the designer to think in a way that addresses all the dimensions of the urban realm. It encourages the collaboration with professionals and experts from other disciplines, namely sociology, psychology, history and philosophy.

The quantum metaphor recognizes the role of the human mind in the creation of the environment, as the end user becomes as much a 'construction unit' as a designer *à part entière* of the city. The professional urbanist ceases to be an 'onlooker from above' and becomes an overseer interfacing between fellow professionals and users; one 'acrobat' amongst many in the quantum urban design team.

New insights as to the *reason* why true traditional environments are invariably more attractive to the city user than modern ones emerge. If the user's true sensitivity is to the embedded *representation of time* and not to form, then alternative ways to embed the sense of time in a new setting can be equally valid – for instance, the quantum hyper-metaphor has room for traditionalists (time in form), ecologists (time in landscape elements) and post-structuralists (time in narrative).

A wonderful characteristic of the quantum metaphor is that it is scalable. The scales of intervention require different models, even if each model uses the same overall metaphor. The risk of repetitive identity is checked by the concept of *diventity* and the accommodation of this variety of models. Additionally, excessive homogenization of architecture at smaller scales is checked by the random personalization of space by its multiple users.

From issues of multicultural education and interdisciplinary collaboration to composition and management of functions, issues of identity and memory, post-war reconstruction and large-scale development phasing, small-scale sensory stimulation to global culture, the hyper-metaphor permits the coexistence of clashing models and theories, and works well at all levels of theory, education and practice. From 'quantum textures' to 'quantum nations', the proposed language replies to one holistic worldview.

In that sense, the language itself is robust, adaptive and universal. Used to its full potential, it can provide the different designers of the urban realm with a simple yet powerful tool that unifies their product without stifling their creativity.

Urban design gains a powerful language with which to approach its subject matter. Using a limited vocabulary with many meanings, and a simple conceptual grammar, the designer can now address a whole range of issues using a single background theory. The result is an environment held together with a strong culture-relevant theme, a scalable unity that has been missed in urban space since traditional cities.

An urban form is thus produced that speaks directly to its users'

perception. Quantum environments *make sense* to their
users because they use the
same simple language at all
scales, a language easily
recognizable by the human
unconscious because it is
similar to the way it really *feels*
the world, and easily perceived
by consciousness since it
reflects how it *knows* the world.

The Greeks spoke of the spirit
of place (*genius loci*), historians of the spirit of time
(*Zeitgeist*), and the Hindus of
the essential spirit of self
(*atman*, like atmosphere) ...
We can now unify these spirits
of space, time and society as
potentiality waves in the SST
continuum.

The modernist city used
zoning to mechanize its

citizens; the postmodern city used rhetoric to make its intellectuals smarter and its citizens dumber. The quantum city uses diventity to make all of its citizens – their minds and their lives – brighter.

We have to describe and to explain a building the upper story of which was erected in the nineteenth century; the ground-floor dates from the sixteenth century, and a careful examination of the masonry discloses the fact that it was reconstructed from a dwelling-tower of the eleventh century. In the cellar we discover Roman foundation walls, and under the cellar a filled-in cave, in the floor of which stone tools are found and remnants of glacial fauna in the layers below. That would be a sort of picture of our mental structure.[3]

Jung uses the metaphor of a layered building to describe our mental structure. How interesting it will be if it turns out that the same metaphor that actually rules our mind can accurately describe our cities. If the human brain truly functions according to quantum processes, then 'quantum concepts of the city' might be exactly what are lacking to tackle man's most ambitious artefact.

More than once while I was

writing the last part of this book some concepts begged to be developed into complete chapters in their own right, as more detailed implications to built form can easily be deduced from the simple caveats of the quantum paradigm. I chose to keep those implications vague and their illustrative examples basic, in spite of the strong temptation to dwell on the potentiality of each, as I fought with the architect in me against his own personal vision. The various issues addressed are therefore used as examples of the adaptability of the quantum language, and most of the

'1001 other concepts' are left to the different readers to imagine.

It is hoped that the basic work undertaken here will be adopted and built upon in future research. The quantum metaphor remains pregnant with possibilities that were only partially addressed here. Its implications on philosophy are tremendous, and it is bound to shape the twenty-first century just as the Cartesian paradigm shaped the twentieth. However, far from any Hegelian interpretations it must be stressed that, unlike previous worldviews where their associated metaphors were unconsciously bred into each individual's education, the dissemination of the new language should now be actively and consciously adopted.

At the time of this writing, it is reported that Christopher Alexander is putting the final touches to his four-volume, 30-years-in-the-making work entitled *The Nature of Order*. According to previews, it tackles the worldview based on the new sciences of the twentieth century, and should be the first major work by an influential architect in the dissemination of the new language. Critics already claim it 'may prove to be one of the most consequential works Oxford has published in all its 500 years'.[4]

Each organized activity or discipline should participate in the creation of a unified framework for thought. Popular and academic literature is slowly but surely shaping the alternative paradigm, through its bringing together again of natural and social sciences. It is

now the role and responsibility of urban design to translate this worldview into real places.

Quantum City provides the first participation of urban

design in an agenda that – it is hoped – might soon become commonplace. In this sense, I chose to call this end chapter 'Transition' and not 'Conclusion'.

It has been 70 years since the development of quantum theory.

Another 70 years from now, different paradigms could be moving us. Teleportation might be a reality, as could be widespread artificial intelligence. We might be colonizing Mars. We could have discovered the secret of creation, or at least of life itself. What would that do to our worldview and to our cities? I do not know. But until then we have this powerful quantum paradigm to work with, so let us.

References

Introduction

1. Peat, F. D. (1994). *Blackfoot Physics*. Fourth Estate Ltd.
2. Orwell, G. (1954). The principles of Newspeak. In: *1984*, p. 241. Penguin.
3. Sennett, R. (1990). *The Conscience of the Eye*, p. 11. Faber & Faber.

Chapter 1 Worldviews and the city

1. Lightman, A. (1994). *Einstein's Dreams*, p. 28. Warner Books.
2. Stanton, M. (2001). A tale of two-and-a-half cities: the urbanism of good (and bad) intentions. Submitted to *Perspecta*, **33**.
3. Jellicoe, G. and Jellicoe, S. (1987). *The Landscape of Man*, p. 129. Thames and Hudson.
4. Zohar, D. (1990). *The Quantum Self*, p. 189. Bloomsbury.
5. Beazley, M. (ed.) (1984). *The World Atlas of Architecture*, p. 161. G. K. Hall & Co.
6. Beazley, M. (ed.) (1984). *The World Atlas of Architecture*, p. 154. G. K. Hall & Co.
7. Sennett, R. (1990). *The Conscience of the Eye*, p. xii. Faber & Faber.
8. Jellicoe, G. and Jellicoe, S. (1987). *The Landscape of Man*, p. 117. Thames and Hudson.
9. Rykwert, J. (1988). *The Idea of a Town: The Anthropology of Urban Form in Rome, Italy and the Ancient World*, p. 90. MIT Press.
10. Madison, J. and Hamilton, A. (1787). *The Federalist Papers*. 7 December, no. 18 (quoted in Johnson, K. B. Sr (2000). *The Power of Story*. www.onejazzstop.com/part_iv_cont.html).

11. Beazley, M. (ed.) (1984). *The World Atlas of Architecture*, pp. 117–19. G. K. Hall & Co.
12. Sennett, R. (1990). *The Conscience of the Eye*, pp. 7–17. Faber & Faber.
13. Kreis, S. (1998). *Lectures on Modern European Intellectual History: The Medieval Worldview.* www.historyguide.org/intellect/lecture2a.html and lecture4a/html.
14. Sennett, R. (1990). *The Conscience of the Eye*, pp. 153–4. Faber & Faber.

Chapter 2 Science and worldviews

1. Zohar, D. (1990). *The Quantum Self*, p. 3. Bloomsbury.
2. Capra, F. (1982). *The Turning Point: Science, Society, and the Rising Culture*, preface. Wildwood House.
3. Prigogine, I. and Stengers, I. (1984). *Order out of* Chaos, p. 7. Heinemann.
4. Prigogine, I. and Stengers, I. (1984). *Order out of Chaos*, p. 37. Heinemann.
5. Merchant, C. (1980). *The Death of Nature*, p. 3. Harper Collins (quoted in Capra, F. (1982). *The Turning Point: Science, Society, and the Rising Culture*, p. 46. Wildwood House).
6. Laing, R. D. (1982). *The Voice of Experience – Experience, Science and Psychiatry*. Penguin Books (quoted in Capra, F. (1982). *The Turning Point: Science, Society, and the Rising Culture*, p. 46. Wildwood House).
7. Capra, F. (1982). *The Turning Point: Science, Society, and the Rising Culture*, pp. 40–41. Wildwood House.
8. Toffler, A. (1984). Science and change. In: Prigogine, I. and Stengers, I. (1984). *Order out of Chaos*, foreword. Heinemann.
9. Kaku, M. (1994). *Hyperspace: A Scientific Odyssey through Parallel Universes, Time Warps, and the 11th Dimension*. Oxford University Press.
10. Kaku, M. (1994). *Hyperspace: A Scientific Odyssey through Parallel Universes, Time Warps, and the 11th Dimension*, p. 84. Oxford University Press.

11. Friedman, A. and Donley, C. (1985) *Einstein as Myth and Muse*. Cambridge University Press.
12. Kaku, M. (1994). *Hyperspace: A Scientific Odyssey through Parallel Universes, Time Warps, and the 11th Dimension*, p. 67. Oxford University Press.
13. Friedman, A. and Donley, C. (1985) *Einstein as Myth and Muse*, pp. 154–76. Cambridge University Press.

Chapter 3 Quantum theory: an introduction to basics

1. Kaku, M. (1994). *Hyperspace: A Scientific Odyssey through Parallel Universes, Time Warps, and the 11th Dimension*. Oxford University Press.
2. Pagels, H. R. (1982). *The Cosmic Code: Quantum Physics as the Language of Nature*, p. 79. Bantam.
3. Kaku, M. (1994). *Hyperspace: A Scientific Odyssey through Parallel Universes, Time Warps, and the 11th Dimension*, p. vii. Oxford University Press.
4. Gribbin, J. (1991). *In Search of Schrödinger's Cat*. Black Swan.
5. Gribbin, J. (1995). *Schrödinger's Kittens*. Weidenfeld & Nicolson.
6. Gribbin, J. (1995). *Schrödinger's Kittens*, pp. 1–9. Weidenfeld & Nicolson.
7. Pagels, H. R. (1982). *The Cosmic Code: Quantum Physics as the Language of Nature*, p. 75. Bantam.
8. Zukav, G. (1979). *The Dancing Wu Li Masters: and Overview of the New Physics*. Rider/Hutchinson.
9. Pagels, H. R. (1982). *The Cosmic Code: Quantum Physics as the Language of Nature*, p. 47. Bantam.
10. Capra, F. (1982). *The Turning Point: Science, Society, and the Rising Culture*, pp. 68–9. Wildwood House.
11. Zohar, D. (1990). *The Quantum Self*, p. 12. Bloomsbury.
12. Zukav, G. (1979). *The Dancing Wu Li Masters: and Overview of the New Physics*, p. 63. Rider/Hutchinson.
13. Pagels, H. R. (1982). *The Cosmic Code: Quantum Physics as the Language of Nature*, p. 241. Bantam.
14. Pagels, H. R. (1982). *The Cosmic Code: Quantum Physics as the Language of Nature*, p. 247. Bantam.

Interlude: Mathematical chaos and urban complexity

1. Batty, M. and Longley, P. (1994). *Fractal Cities*, pp. v–vi Academic Press.
2. Mandelbrot, B. (1983). *The Fractal Geometry of Nature*. Freeman.
3. Bovill, C. (1996). *Fractal Geometry in Architecture and Design*. Birkhauser.
4. Gleick, J. (1987). *Chaos: Making a New Science*. Heinemann Ltd.
5. Abel, C. (2000). *Architecture and Identity: Responses to Cultural and Technological Change*. Butterworth-Heinemann.
6. De Landa, M. (2000). *A Thousand Years of Nonlinear History*. Zone Books/Swerve Editions.
7. Nørretranders, T. (1998). *The User Illusion: Cutting Consciousness Down to Size*. Penguin.
8. Zohar, D. and Marshall, I. (1995). *The Quantum Society*. Bloomsbury.
9. Jencks, C. (1998). *The Architecture of the Jumping Universe*. Wiley.

Chapter 4 The quantum worldview

1. Mumford, L. (1934). *Technics and Civilization*. Harcourt Brace & World.
2. Giedon, S. (1948). *Mechanization takes Command: A Contribution to Anonymous History*. W. W. Norton & Co.
3. Zohar, D. (1990). *The Quantum Self*. Bloomsbury.
4. Zohar, D. and Marshall, I. (1995). *The Quantum Society*. Bloomsbury.
5. Hartwell, A. (1995). Scientific ideas and education in the 21st century. In: *The 21st Century Learning Initiative*. www.newhorizons.org/ofc_21cliash.html.
6. Prigogine, I. and Stengers, I. (1984). *Order out of Chaos*, p. 37. Heinemann.
7. Popper, K. and Eccles, J. (1983). *The Self and its Brain*. Routledge & Kegan Paul.

8. Nagel, T. (1979). *Mortal Questions*. Cambridge University Press.

Interlude: *Feng shui or the Tao of the city*

1. Ko, A. (1998). A Feng Shui Approach to Urban Design. Unpublished MA Dissertation, JCUD, Oxford Brookes University.
2. Jellicoe, G. and Jellicoe, S. (1987). *The Landscape of Man*, p. 68. Thames and Hudson.
3. Lovelock, J. (1982). *Gaïa*. Oxford University Press.
4. Capra, F. (1976). *The Tao of Physics*. Wildwood House.
5. Peat, F. D. and Briggs, I. (1990). *Turbulent Mirror: An Illustrated Guide to Chaos, Theory and the Science of Wholeness*. Fourth Estate.
6. Peat, F. D. (1994). *Blackfoot Physics*. Fourth Estate.

Chapter 5 *20th century cities*

1. *Encyclopedia Britannica*. The Nature of Modern Society. CD edition 1997.
2. Le Corbusier. (1929). The City of to-morrow and its planning. In: *The City Reader* (R. Legates and F. Stout, eds), p. 375. Routledge.
3. Jellicoe, G. and Jellicoe, S. (1987). *The Landscape of Man*, p. 287. Thames and Hudson.
4. LeGates, R. and Stout, F. (eds) (1996). *The City Reader*, p. 377. Routledge.
5. Jacobs, J. (1961). *The Death and Life of Great American Cities*. Vintage Books.
6. Venturi, R. (1966). Complexity and contradiction in architecture. In: *Theories and Manifestos of Contemporary Architecture* (C. Jencks and K. Kropf, eds). Academy Editions.
7. Jencks,C. and Kropf, K. (eds) (1993). *Theories and Manifestos of Contemporary Architecture*. Academy Editions.
8. Papadakis, A., Cooke, C. and Benjamin, A. (1989). *Deconstruction (Omnibus Volume)*. Academy Editions.

9. Papadakis, A. and Watson, H. (1990). *New Classicism (Omnibus Volume)*. Academy Editions.
10. Porphyros, D. (1984). *Leon Krier*, p. 15. AD Editions.
11. Kelbaugh, D. (1997). *Common Place: toward Neighborhood and Regional Design*. University of Washington Press.
12. Papadakis, A. and Watson, H. (1990). *New Classicism (Omnibus Volume)*, p. 203. Academy Editions.

Interlude: Cities and worldviews and cinema

1. Economakis, R. (ed.) (1993). New practice in urban design. *AD Profile*, 105. Architectural Design.

Chapter 6 Urban design and the quantum worldview

1. Zohar, D. and Marshall, I. (1995). *The Quantum Society*, p. 189. Bloomsbury.
2. Whitehead, S. N. (1967). *Science and the Modern World*. Free Press (quoted in Hartwell, A. (1995). Scientific ideas and education in the 21st century. In: *The 21st Century Learning Initiative*. www.newhorizons.org/ofc_21cliash.html).
3. Prigogine, I. and Stengers, I. (1984). *Order Out of Chaos*, p. 295. Heinemann.
4. Koolhaas, R and Mau, B. (1995). *S, M, L, XL*, p. 969. The Monacelli Press.
5. Department of the Environment (1995). *Quality in Town and Country – The Urban Design Campaign*. HMSO.
6. Department of the Environment and RICS (1996). *Quality of Urban Design – A Study of the Involvement of Private Property Decision-Makers in Urban Design*. HMSO.
7. Carmona (1996). Controlling Urban Design – Part 1. Journal of Urban Design, **1**, **(1)**, p. 4.
8. Rowley, A. (1994). Definitions of urban design: the nature and concerns of urban design. *Planning Practice and Research*, **9 (3)**.
9. Jones, C. (1980). *Design Methods: Seeds for Human Futures*. Wiley.

10. Myers, D. and Kitsuse, A. (2000). Constructing the future in planning: a survey of theories and tools. *Journal of Planning Education and Research*, **29,** 221–31.

11. Koolhaas, R and Mau, B. (1995). *S, M, L, XL,* p. 967. The Monacelli Press.

12. Sennett, R. (1990). *The Conscience of the Eye*, p. 170. Faber & Faber.

13. de Portzamparc, C. (1996). *Portzamparc*. Birkhauser Architectural.

14. de Portzamparc, C. (1997). *Genealogie des Formes*. Distributed Art Publishers.

15. Panerai, P. (1997). *Formes Urbaines de l'Ilot à la Barre*. Editions Parenthèses (Diasporales).

16. Panerai, P. (1999). *Analyse Urbaine*. Editions Parenthèses.

17. Koolhaas, R. (1978). *Delirious New York*. The Monacelli Press.

18. Koolhaas, R and Mau, B. (1995). *S, M, L, XL,* p. 967. The Monacelli Press.

19. Koolhaas, R., Boeri, S., Kwinter, S. *et al.* (2000). *Mutations*. Actar.

20. Hilgemeier, M. (1993). *One Metaphor Fits All*. www.is-bremen.de/~mhi/fvcad_09.htm

21. Calvino, I. (1997). *Mr Palomar*. Minerva.

22. Calvino, I. (1997). *Mr Palomar*, pp. 97–100. Minerva.

23. Hall, P. (1996). The city of theory. In: *The City Reader* (R. Legates and F. Stout, eds), p. 383. Routledge.

Chapter 7 A quantum look to the postgraduate education and practice of urbanism

1. Peat, F. D. (1994). *Blackfoot Physics*, p. 231. Fourth Estate Ltd.

2. Centro Internazionale Di Studi Sul Disegno Urbano (1992). *European Charter for the City*. Council of Europe.

3. Jacobs, S. and Appleyard, D. (1996). Towards an urban design manifesto. In: *The City Reader* (R. Legates and F. Stout, eds), p. 169. Routledge.

4. Zohar, D. and Marshall, I. (1995). *The Quantum Society*, p. 78. Bloomsbury.

5. Kelbaugh, D. (1997). *Common Place: Toward Neighborhood and Regional Design*. University of Washington Press.

6. MG Taylor Corporation (1997). *A Model for Releasing Group Genius.* www.MGTaylor.com/MGTaylor/glasbead/axioms.htm.

7. MG Taylor Corporation (1997). *Looping and Leaping: Quantum Mechanics and the Stages of an Enterprise.* www.MGTaylor.com/MGTaylor.

8. MG Taylor Corporation (1997). *A Model for Releasing Group Genius.* www.MGTaylor.com/MGTaylor/jotm/architec.htm.

9. MG Taylor Corporation (1997). *A Model for Releasing Group Genius.* www.MGTaylor.com/MGTaylor/glasbead/dbumodel.htm.

10. Brand, S. (1994). *How Buildings Learn: What Happens After They're Built,* pp. 178–83. Viking.

11. Zohar, D. (1997). *Rewiring the Corporate Brain,* p. 57. Berrett-Koehler Publishers.

12. Brand, S. (1994). *How Buildings Learn: What Happens After They're Built.* Viking.

13. Zohar, D. (1997). *Rewiring the Corporate Brain,* p. 65. Berrett-Koehler Publishers.

14. Myers, D. and Kitsuse, A. (2000). Constructing the future in planning: a survey of theories and tools. *Journal of Planning Education and Research,* **29,** 221–31.

15. Ornstein, R. and Ehrlich, P. (1991). *New World, New Mind: Changing the Way We Think to Save Our* Future. Paladin.

16. Nørretranders, T. (1998). *The User Illusion: Cutting Consciousness Down to Size,* p. 413. Penguin Press.

Chapter 8 Quantum analysis of the urban realm

1. Koolhaas, R. and Mau, B. (1995). *S, M, L, XL,* p. 969. The Monacelli Press.

2. Krier, R. (1979). *Urban Space.* Academy Editions.

3. Hillier, B. and Hanson, J. (1987). *The Social Logic of Space,* p. 29. Cambridge University Press.

4. Hillier, B. and Hanson, J. (1987). *The Social Logic of Space.* Cambridge University Press.

5. Alexander, C. (1965). The city is not a tree. In: *The City Reader* (R. Legates and F. Stout, eds), pp. 119–20. Routledge.

6. Penrose, R. (1987). *The Emperor's New Mind*. Vintage.

7. Zohar, D. (1990). *The Quantum Self*. Bloomsbury.

8. Zohar, D. and Marshall, I. (2000). *SQ: Connecting with our Spiritual Intelligence*. Bloomsbury.

9. Salingaros, N. (1997). *Remarks on a City's Composition*. www.math.utsa.edu/sphere/salingar/remarkscity.htm

10. Brand, S. (1994). *How Buildings Learn: What Happens After They're Built*. Viking.

11. Mumford, L. (1937). What is a city? In: *The City Reader* (R. Legates and F. Stout, eds), p. 183. Routledge.

12. Prigogine, I. and Stengers, I. (1984). *Order Out of Chaos*. Heinemann.

13. Pike, B. (1981). The image of the city in modern literature. In: *The City Reader* (R. Legates and F. Stout, eds), p. 243. Routledge.

14. Anders, P. (1998). Cybrids.*Convergence*, **4(1),** 80–90.

15. Salingaros, N. (1999). Urban space and its information field. *Journal of Urban Design*, **4,** 29–49.

16. Ellis, H. C. and Reed Hunt, R. (1993). *Fundamentals of Cognitive Psychology*, 5th edn. McGraw Hill.

17. Duhl, L. J. (1963). *The Urban Condition*. Basic Books.

18. Holahan, C. (1982). *Environmental Psychology*. Random House.

19. Lynch, K. (1960). The city image and its elements. In: *The City Reader* (R. Legates and F. Stout, eds), p. 99. Routledge.

20. Zohar, D. (1990). *The Quantum Self*, pp. 187–88. Bloomsbury.

Chapter 9 Implications for built form

1. Pike, B. (1981). The image of the city in modern literature. In: *The City Reader* (R. Legates and F. Stout, eds), p. 243. Routledge.

2. Milizia, F. (1813). *Principi di Architettura Civile*, 3rd edn, Vol. II, pp. 26–28 (quoted in Tafuri, M. (1976). *Architecture and Utopia*, pp. 20–21. MIT Press).

3. Prigogine, I. and Stengers, I. (1984). *Order out of Chaos*. Heinemann.

4. Brand, S. (1994). *How Buildings Learn: What Happens After They're Built*, p. 189. Viking.
5. Holahan, C. (1982). *Environmental Psychology*. Random House.
6. Bohm, D. (1980). *Wholeness and The Implicate Order*. Routledge & Kegan Paul.
7. Bohm, D. (1985). *Unfolding Meaning: a Weekend of Dialogue with David Bohm*. ARK Paperbacks.
8. Bohm, D. (1994). *Thought as a System*. Routledge.
9. Zohar, D. (1990). *The Quantum Self*. Bloomsbury.
10. Bentley, I., McGlynn, S. and Smith, G. (1985). *Responsive Environments*. Butterworth Architectural.
11. Salingaros, N. (1998). Theory of the urban web. *Journal of Urban Design*, **3**, 53–71, and www.math.utsa.edu/sphere/salingar/UrbanSpace.html
12. Alexander, C. (1979). The city is not a tree. In: *The City Reader* (R. Legates and F. Stout, eds). Routledge.
13. Hillier, B. and Hanson, J. (1987). *The Social Logic of Space*, p. 57. Cambridge University Press.
14. Ellis, H. C. and Reed Hunt, R. (1993). *Fundamentals of Cognitive Psychology*, 5th edn. McGraw Hill.
15. English Partnerships and The Housing Corporation. (2001). *Urban Design* Compendium. Llewelyn-Davies.
16. Ko, A. (1998). A Feng Shui Approach to Urban Design. Unpublished MA Dissertation, JCUD, Oxford Brookes University.
17. Alexander, C., Neis, H., Anninou, A. and King, I. (1987). *A New Theory of Urban Design*, pp. 60–61. Oxford University Press.
18. Tabet, J. (1997). International Symposium of Postwar Reconstruction, Beirut.
19. Venturi, R., Scott-Brown, D. and Izenour, S. (1972). Learning from Las Vegas. In: *Theories and Manifestos of Contemporary Architecture* (C. Jencks and K. Kropf, eds). Academy Editions.
20. Zohar, D. and Marshall, I. (1995). *SQ: Connecting with our Spiritual Intelligence*, pp. 147–51. Bloomsbury.
21. Jencks, C. (1995). *The Architecture of the Jumping Universe*. Academy Editions.
22. Krier, L. (1984). Houses, palaces, cities. In: *AD Profile* (D. Porphyrios, ed.), p. 54. Architectural Design.

Transition

1. de Portzamparc, C. (1996). *Portzamparc*, p. 62. Birkhauser Architectural.
2. Koolhaus, R. and Mau, B. (1995). *S, M, L, XL*. The Monacelli Press.
3. Jung, C. J. (1994). Contributions to analytical psychology. Quoted in *Architecture and Urbanism*, **June,** 23.
4. William McClung, special project editor for Oxford University Press, former senior editor of the University of California Press. Quoted in Salingaros.
5. Salingaros, N. (1997). *Remarks on a City's Composition*. www.math.utsa.edu/sphere/salingar/NatureofOrder.html reviews.

Further reading

Abram, D. (1996). *The Spell of The Sensuous*. Pantheon Books.

Alexander, C., Ishikawa, S., Silverstein, M., *et al.* (1977). *A Pattern Language*. Oxford University Press.

Barzun, J. (1992). *The Columbia History of The World*. Harper & Row.

Bateson, G. (1979). *Mind and Nature*. Dutton.

Beck, U. (1994). *Reflexive Modernization: Politics, Tradition and Aesthetics In The Modern Society*. Polity Press.

Bell, J. S. (1988). *Speakable and Unspeakable In Quantum Mechanics*. Cambridge University Press.

Bouratinos, E. (1992). Interpersonal democracy: the quantum approach. In: *Proceedings of Political Philosophy Today: Considerations after the End of Communism*. University of Crete.

Briggs, J. and Peat, F. D. (1989). *Turbulent Mirror*. Harper & Row.

Bückle, S. and Sakschewski, T. (1997). *Beirut–Berlin*. Exhibition Catalogue.

Calvino, I. (1974). *Invisible Cities*. Harcourt Brace Jovanovitch.

Capra, F. (1996). *The Web of Life: A New Synthesis of Mind and Matter*. Harper Collins.

Carroll, L. (1965). *Through the Looking Glass*. Dent.

Chauprade, A. and Renaut, T. (not dated). *Beyrouth Eternelle: Portrait d'une Ville à l'Esprit Présérvé*. Collection Villes Eternelles. ASA Editions.

Duffy, F. (1992). *The Changing Workplace*. Phaidon.

Eisenmann, P. (1994). Confronting the Double Zeitgeist. *Architecture,* **October,** 51.

Fanstein, S. and Campbell, S. (eds) (1996). *Readings in Urban Theory*. Blackwell.

Friedman, D. (1988). *Florentine New Towns: Urban Design in the Middle Ages*. MIT Press.

Gablik, S. (1984). *Has Modernism Failed?* Thames & Hudson.

Giddens, A. (1990). *The Consequences of Modernity.* Blackwell.

Graham, S. and Marvin, S. (1996). *Telecommunications and the City.* Routledge.

Harvey, D. (1990). *The Condition of Postmodernity.* Basil Blackwell.

Hawking, S. (1996). *The Illustrated Brief History of Time.* BCA.

Heisenberg, W. (1963). *Physics and Philosophy.* Allen & Unwin.

Herbert, N. (1997). *Quantum Tantra.* mail.cruzio.com/~quanta/qtantra1.html.

Jencks, C. (1993). *Heteropolis.* Academy Editions.

Jencks, C. (ed.) (1998). *New Science – New Architecture?* Academy Editions.

Kosko, B. (1994). *Fuzzy Thinking.* Flamingo.

Krier, R. (1979). *Urban Space.* Academy Editions.

Kroll, L. (1983). The architecture of complexity. In *Theories and Manifestos of Contemporary Architecture* (C. Jencks and K. Kropf, eds). Academy Editions.

Kuhn, T. (1962). *The Structure of Scientific Revolutions.* University of Chicago Press.

Kuhn, T. (1977). *The Essential Tension.* University of Chicago Press.

Lightman, A. (1992). *Great Ideas in Physics.* McGraw Hill.

Lightman, A. (1996). *Dance for Two.* Bloomsbury.

Lockwood, M. (1990). *Mind, Brain and the Quantum.* Basil Blackwell.

Lynch, K. (1972). *What Time Is This Place?* MIT Press.

Marshall, I. (1991). *Some Phenomenological Implications of a Quantum Model of Consciousness. Where Does 'I' Come From?* Conference Proceedings. SUNY.

Merleau-Ponty, M. (1962). *Phenomenology of Perception.* Humanities Press.

Moudon, A. (1986). *Built for Change.* MIT Press.

Nagel, T. (1995). *Other Minds.* Oxford University Press.

Nifle, R. (1996). *La Trialectique: Sujet-Objet-Projet.* www.institut-coherences.fr/ECRITS/TEXTES/DOCUMENT/trial.htm

Penrose, R. (1987). Minds, machines, and mathematics. In: *Mindwaves* (C. Blakemore and S. Greenfield, eds). Basil Blackwell.

Penrose, R. (1994). *Shadows of the Mind: A Search for the Missing Science of Consciousness.* Oxford University Press.

Penrose, R. and Hawking, S. (1996). *The Nature of Space and Time.* Princeton University Press.

Penrose, R. and Isham C. J. (eds). (1986). *Quantum Concepts in Space and Time.* Clarendon.

Pinker, S. (1985). *Visual Cognition.* MIT Press.

Pinker, S. (1988). *Connections and Symbols.* MIT Press.

Pinker, S. (1994). *The Language Instinct: The New Science of Language and Mind.* Allen Lane.

Rahim, A. (ed.) (2000). Contemporary processes in architecture. *Architectural Design*, **70(3).** Wiley-Academy.

Redhead, M. (1987). *Incompleteness, Nonlocality, and Realism.* Clarendon Press.

Reed, E. and Ajami, F. (1988). *Beirut: City of Regrets.* W. W. Norton & Co.

Rowe, P.G. and Sarkis, H. (eds). (1998). *Projecting Beirut: Episodes in the Construction and Reconstruction of a Modern City.* Prestel.

Rykwert, J. (2000). *The Seduction of Place.* Weidenfeld & Nicolson.

Salingaros, N. (2000). Complexity and urban coherence. *Journal of Urban Design*, **5,** 291–316.

Schuiten, F. and Peeters, B. (1996). *Les Cités Obscures: Le Guide des Cités.* Casterman.

Schwartz, P. (1991). *The Art of The Long View.* Doubleday.

Scruton, R. (1995). *A Short History of Modern Philosophy*, 2nd edn. Routledge.

Sennett, R. (1973). *The Uses of Disorder: Personal Identity and City Life.* Penguin.

Sennett, R. (1992). Flesh and stone: the body and the city. *Times Literary Supplement*, 18 September, p. 3.

Skarda, C. and Freeman, W. (1987). How brains make chaos in order to make sense of the world. *Behavioral and Brain Sciences*, **10(2),** 161–73.

Stryker, M. P. (1989). Is grandmother an oscillation? *Nature*, **338**, 297–8.

Teller, P. (1986). Relational holism and quantum mechanics. *British Journal for The Philosophy of Science*, **37**.

Tranick, R. (1986). *Finding Lost Space.* Van Nostrand Reinhold.

Tuan, Yi-Fu. (1974). *Topophilia: a Study of Environmental Perception, Attitudes, and Values*. Prentice-Hall.

Weber, E. (1986). The pleasures of diversity. *Times Literary Supplement*, 22 August, p. 906.

Westwood, S. and Williams, J. (eds). (1997). *Imagining Cities: Scripts, Signs, Memories*. Routledge.

Wortheim, M. (1999). *The Pearly Gates of Cyberspace*. Random House.

Index